To: _____

From: _____

Date: _____

30 Stories for Girls with God-Sized Dreams

DaySpring

LIVE YOUR FAITH

30 Stories for Girls with God-Sized Dreams
© 2019 DaySpring Cards, Inc. All rights reserved.
First Edition, November 2019

Published by:

P.O. Box 1010
Siloam Springs, AR 72761
dayspring.com

Illustrators: Amber Roderick, Jon Huckeby, and Hannah Skelton

Produced with the assistance of Peachtree Publishing Services.

Contributing writer: April LoTempio

Printed in China
Prime: J1593
ISBN: 978-1-64454-442-6

Contents

HARRIET TUBMAN

Activist (1820–1913)

A Champion for Freedom

Can you imagine traveling at night with only the stars to guide you? What if you had to walk for miles in the darkness with a group of people, trying to escape your captors? You would have to be quiet, because if you were caught, you would return to a life of bondage or even face death. Would you be brave enough to continue? Would you trust God to help you? Harriet Tubman chose bravery. She lived when many African Americans were slaves, and she worked hard to deliver people from slavery.

Slaves were owned by masters who could force them to work all hours of the day or beat them for any small mistake. Slaves had no choice but to obey. What a terrible life! Harriet's parents were slaves, so she entered this life from the very beginning along with her brothers and sisters. Sometimes slave owners would take children from their parents, and at any time, a family could be separated when a mom, dad, or child was sold to a plantation far away.

Harriet didn't have a regular childhood like you and me. She lived a difficult life filled with abuse and hard work. She spent much of her time rented out to neighboring fields and farms. She also didn't go to school and never learned to read or write. But Harriet heard Bible stories full of encouraging messages about God's love and comfort, and God's words helped Harriet in times of need.

Once, a slave owner threw a heavy metal weight that hit Harriet in the head. This caused her to have seizures, headaches, and sudden sleepiness all her life. This injury could have been deadly, but God had bigger plans for Harriet. In fact, the injury caused her to have visions, which she believed were from God.

When Harriet's owner died, she worried that she would be sold and have to leave her family. She and two of her brothers decided to escape and head to Philadelphia, Pennsylvania, where they could live as free people. No one would own them or force them to work. However, her brothers changed their minds. They were afraid of being captured and punished, so Harriet escaped alone.

"I don't know where to go or what to do, but I expect You to lead me."

It would have been easy for Harriet to get lost or captured during her ninety-mile journey. Thankfully, she got help from the Underground Railroad: a network of free people who helped runaway slaves. Harriet followed their trails until she reached Philadelphia and her freedom. God protected her even in the midst of danger.

Soon, Harriet learned that some of her family members were going to be sold. She snuck back into Maryland to help them escape. Harriet showed such bravery! Her family needed her, so she put aside any fear and helped them find freedom. Again and again, Harriet returned to the South to help more enslaved people. Each trip grew riskier as more people were after Harriet. They wanted to stop her from helping slaves.

A new law made matters worse for Harriet. Any escaped slave found in the North had to be returned to the South. Philadelphia was no longer safe, so Harriet led others all the way to Canada. She even disguised herself—sometimes as an old woman or as a man—to avoid getting caught!

How did Harriet find the courage to make these dangerous journeys? She trusted God. She told God, "I don't know where to go or what to do, but I expect You to lead me." And God always led her. People saw Harriet as a modern-day Moses. Moses, with God's help, led the Israelites out of slavery in Egypt. Harriet fought against slavery by bringing slaves to freedom.

During the Civil War, the North fought against the South to unite the nation and end slavery. During this time, Harriet worked as a cook, a nurse, a scout, and a spy. She even guided Union forces to free more than seven hundred slaves, making her the first woman to do anything like this in the Civil War. When the war ended, Harriet settled in New York and worked hard to help elderly people, former slaves, and women.

Harriet eventually died of pneumonia, and she was buried with military honors. Her dedication to bringing people to freedom inspires us to be brave despite difficult circumstances.

PRAYER

Dear God, thank You for Harriet Tubman's inspirational life. Thank You for protecting me and giving me courage when I need it. Help me to bravely help other people. Amen.

FLORENCE NIGHTINGALE
Nurse (1820–1910)
Compassionate Servant

Do you know what you want to be when you grow up? Not everyone does at an early age, but God has designed each one of us with at least one special talent. God gave Florence Nightingale the gift of helping others. With God's help, Florence dedicated her life to helping sick people. Her influence forever changed the way people practice medicine today.

Florence grew up in a very wealthy family. Her father made sure that she was well educated, and she learned many subjects, including Latin, Greek, French, history, and math. Young ladies at that time were expected to get married to rich and important men and raise a family. Florence, however, realized that God had a different plan for her. She wanted to help sick and poor people. When she was just seventeen years old, she wrote, "God spoke to me and called me to His service."

But when Florence shared her dream to pursue nursing, her family disapproved. Nursing was not considered an acceptable job for a young woman. Yet Florence knew this was what she was supposed to do. She continued to help sick and poor people who lived in a nearby village.

Waiting is not easy, but God sometimes has us wait because He has a perfect plan for us. Florence had to wait several years before she could be trained in nursing, but she eventually enrolled in a school in Germany. Returning to England a few years later, Florence got a job at a hospital, where she was quickly promoted to superintendent. When the Crimean War broke out shortly afterward, Florence gathered a group of nurses and sailed to Crimea in Eastern Europe to help sick and wounded soldiers.

The conditions left Florence shocked and saddened when she arrived. More soldiers were dying from the spread of disease inside the hospital than from battle injuries. A nearby cesspool caused the water to be contaminated. Patients lay in their own filth. Rats and bugs infested every room. The hospital lacked help, and medical supplies were low. Florence later recalled, "Beggars in the streets of London were at that time leading the lives of princes compared to the life of our soldiers in the Crimea when I arrived on the scene with thirty-six nurses."

Because of Florence, nursing grew into an honorable career for women.

What would you have done under such conditions? Would you have given up because it seemed almost impossible to make things right? Florence didn't give up. She was dedicated to helping those in need. She knew God called her to this task.

Right away, Florence got to work. She enlisted patients who were well enough to clean the inside of the hospital. She created a kitchen that allowed healthy meals to be prepared for patients who could only eat certain foods. She set up laundry services so they would have clean linens. She even started a library so that patients could pass the time reading. Her patients nicknamed her "the Lady with the Lamp" because she would often carry a lamp as she worked late into the night, tending to the wounded.

With the changes that Florence made, the death rate in the hospital dropped! Many men were now living instead of dying. Using her experiences, Florence wrote a report for the British Army that explained how to improve hospitals. It caused major changes in the way hospitals around the world were run from then on. After the war, Florence returned home to a hero's welcome. The Queen presented her with a valuable brooch and prize money. Florence used the money to help sick people. She established St. Thomas' Hospital and the Nightingale Training School for Nurses. Because of Florence, nursing grew into an honorable career for women.

While in Crimea, Florence had received an infection that left her in poor health. Despite this, she wrote books and papers about the proper way to run hospitals. From her bed, Florence conducted interviews and welcomed important visitors. She even gave advice during the American Civil War on how to manage field hospitals.

Florence died at the age of ninety. She at one time said, "It is such a blessing to have been called, however unworthy, to be the handmaid of the Lord." Florence inspires us to find our gifts and use them to serve God.

PRAYER

Dear God, thank You for giving me a unique gift. Help me to learn more about the way You made me so I can use that gift to help people. Amen.

MOTHER TERESA
Nun (1910–1997)
Selfless Service

What if God asked you to give up everything you have to live a life wholly devoted to others? What if those people were the poorest of the poor? Mother Teresa gave her life to serve God by helping poor, sick, and lonely people in India.

Mother Teresa's real name was Agnes Gonxha Bojaxhiu. She was born in Macedonia, a country north of Greece. Her family valued faith, and even though they weren't rich, her mother always found ways to help the poor people in their town.

When Agnes turned eighteen, she decided to become a missionary. A missionary is a person who shares God's love by helping and serving others. She joined the Sisters of Loreto, who had missions in India, and took the name Sister Teresa.

Before leaving for India, Sister Teresa spent six weeks learning English. After she arrived in India, she continued to study English and also learned Bengali and Hindi. In Calcutta, Sister Teresa began teaching girls at St. Mary's High School. She believed that education helped people escape from poverty.

After several years, Sister Teresa took her final vows as a nun, promising to live a life of poverty, chastity, and obedience. When she became the principal of the school, she took the name Mother Teresa.

Mother Teresa knew God called her to serve as a nun. But while on her way to a retreat, she heard Jesus tell her to leave her school and work directly with the people living in the slums of Calcutta—the poorest and most run-down parts of the city. Although Mother Teresa wanted to serve there, she had to get special permission from the church before she could go.

It took two years to get permission, and the church only granted Mother Teresa a one-year trial period. With just a bit of medical training and a few pennies in her pocket, Mother Teresa stepped into the worst slums of the city to minister to people who were poor, sick, unwanted, and unseen.

Mother Teresa devoted her life to showing God's love to sick and poor people.

She started by teaching a few children their letters. This led to more children participating, and then people began donating items to help. As an incentive to learn, Mother Teresa offered the children bars of soap when they came to class. When the trial year ended, the church granted Mother Teresa extended time to serve.

Mother Teresa had to completely trust God for her needs. She didn't even have a place to stay when she first started. But over time, God's faithfulness grew apparent. Graduates from St. Mary's and other people started helping her in her work; this led her to start an organization called Missionaries of Charity. When she asked the local government for a place to start a home for people who were dying, she was given an abandoned building. God gave her an overlooked building to provide shelter and care for overlooked people.

She started an orphanage and centers for blind, disabled, and elderly people. She also helped people who were sick with leprosy. In time, the Missionaries of Charity grew to more than four thousand members in more than ninety countries. Through a documentary filmed about her work, Mother Teresa received donations from people all over the world that helped to support the ministry.

Mother Teresa devoted her life to showing God's love to sick and poor people. Organizations in many countries recognized her efforts. Despite all the attention she received, she remained humble. She said, "By blood, I am Albanian. By citizenship, an Indian. By faith, I am a Catholic nun. As to my calling, I belong to the world. As to my heart, I belong entirely to the Heart of Jesus."

She died at eighty-seven years of age.

Mother Teresa inspires us to help people in need, no matter who they are.

PRAYER

Dear God, You have a calling for each one of us. For Mother Teresa, it was to serve the poorest of the poor. Help me to recognize how best I can serve You, and help me to trust You always. Amen.

MAYA ANGELOU

Poet, Author (1928–2014)

A Woman of Wonderful Words

Do you enjoy reading a good book? Perhaps you like mysteries or adventure stories. Or maybe you like poetry or classics. There once was a girl named Maya who loved books of all kinds, and she eventually grew up to write her own stories.

Maya Angelou was born on April 4, 1928, in St. Louis, Missouri. Her birth name was actually Marguerite, but her brother had a habit of calling her "Mya Sister," which eventually became "Maya." When she and her brother were only three and four years of age, they took a train all by themselves to live with their grandma in Arkansas.

Perhaps going to live with her grandmother was the very best thing for Maya. For it was during that time that she was taught to read by one of her uncles. Instantly, she fell in love with books and the adventures on which they took her.

When Maya turned seven, she was sent back to live with her mother. Sadly, her mother's boyfriend was not a nice person. He hurt Maya. At first, she was afraid to tell her mother, but then, she bravely spoke up about what had happened. Maya did the right thing by speaking up!

However, not long after that, her mother's boyfriend was killed. In young Maya's mind, she blamed herself, even though she had nothing to do with it. This terrified Maya, and she did not say a word for five whole years!

Fortunately, a kind teacher named Bertha Flowers helped Maya overcome her fear and her silence. She encouraged Maya to read and to speak. Mrs. Flowers also introduced Maya to poetry from famous authors such as Edgar Allan Poe and Charles Dickens.

Maya finished high school in California and took an interest in singing, dancing, and acting. She had the opportunity to travel overseas to perform in an opera! She was quite good at dancing and acting, but as she got older, she became more involved with politics and speaking on behalf of people's rights.

Maya had a wonderful way of expressing things that flowed from her pen to the page.

Working with important people such as Martin Luther King Jr. and Malcolm X, Maya took a stand for people who were mistreated because of the color of their skin. She knew that all people had been created by a loving God and that He did not want people to fight about whether they were brown, black, or white. Over the course of Maya's life, she made more than eighty speeches for the rights of her fellow African Americans. That's a lot of speeches!

Through every stage of life, Maya continued to read books and write fervently—that is, with lots of energy and passion. She mostly wrote poems and plays, but one time, at a dinner party, she began sharing her life's story. The people who heard it encouraged her to write her story down and make it into a book. Maya took their advice and wrote her first book.

Her first book, *I Know Why the Caged Bird Sings*, became a best seller and opened many doors for her. While some of Maya's books were about her life, others were beautiful works of poetry. In fact, her poetry is now used for teaching literature in schools and universities all over the United States. Maya had a wonderful way of expressing things that flowed from her pen to the page. She was even invited to read one of her poems at a presidential inauguration in 1993—the day Bill Clinton was officially made president of the United States.

On May 28, 2014, at eighty-six years of age, Maya Angelou passed away. Many people all over the world payed tribute to her life, including former US presidents Bill Clinton and Barack Obama. They remembered her for being a wonderful and talented woman who made a big difference in the world.

Maya Angelou's legacy lives on through her stories, her poems, and the words she used to bless people all over the world.

PRAYER

Dear God, thank You for kind and loving people in this world like Maya Angelou, who wrote beautiful words for others to read. Help me to always speak words that are kind and to write words that will encourage others. Amen.

CATHERINE BOOTH

Cofounder of the Salvation Army (1829–1890)

Army Mother for the Lord

What if you lived in a time when women could not teach from the Bible? What if you felt that God was calling you to speak about Him? Would you obey? Catherine Booth obeyed. She was a preacher's wife who was passionate about telling people about Jesus.

Catherine grew up in England in a family that loved God. Her father occasionally served as a preacher, and her mother encouraged strong moral behavior. Catherine shared her parents' deep faith, and by the time she was twelve, she had read the Bible eight times!

As a teenager, a spinal problem forced Catherine to stay in bed for months at a time. But as a voracious reader, Catherine used that time to read books by writers such as John Wesley and Charles Finney— men who loved God. Their thoughts and teachings about the Bible greatly influenced her. Catherine's experience with illness shows that God sometimes uses hardships to strengthen our character.

Catherine felt that God wanted her to teach people the Bible through preaching, an uncommon path for women in England at that time. She met and married a preacher named William Booth. They shared a passion for teaching the Bible and serving people in need. William, however, felt that women should not be preachers. Catherine did not agree with him, but she respected his beliefs. She wrote a short but powerful book on the subject of women in ministry. In it, she argued for the equality of men and women before God. She explained that God's forgiveness is for both men and women.

One day, while sitting in church and listening to William preach, Catherine felt a sudden urgency to speak. Although she feared making a fool of herself, she walked up to the pulpit, told her husband that she wanted to speak, and then shared what was on her heart. She said, "I dare say many of you have been looking on me as a very devout woman, but I have been disobeying God. I am convinced that women have the right and duty to speak up; yes, even to preach! I have struggled with this for a long time, but I'll struggle with it no longer." When she finished, the audience was astounded. From then on, Catherine did not ignore God's call to preach.

"I don't believe in any religion apart from doing the will of God."

William and Catherine preached to poor people, the homeless, and the forgotten on the streets. They trained other preachers and started the mission that became the Salvation Army. Through their preaching, many people—even drunkards and thieves—started to love God, and their lives were changed. Catherine began preaching more and more as her reputation spread and demand for her preaching grew.

The Salvation Army grew, with many of the first members becoming preachers themselves. They preached and sang in the streets of London, sharing the power of God through their messages. Sometimes they were arrested for preaching in public places. The Church of England opposed the Salvation Army partly because it gave women equal status with men.

Despite opposition, the Salvation Army continued working to help people and tell them about God. In a few short years, more than 250,000 people believed in Jesus because of the Salvation Army. Catherine began to organize food shops where the poor could buy cheap but filling meals. On holidays, she would cook and deliver three hundred meals to the poor. When her husband became ill, Catherine also took over administrative duties of the Salvation Army. She did all this while raising eight children!

Catherine's gentle but powerful preaching about the Bible inspired hundreds of women to follow in her footsteps. These "Hallelujah lasses" helped make the Salvation Army one of the most effective missions in England. All eight of the Booth children became active leaders in the Salvation Army as well. The organization spread around the world and is now operating in one hundred countries. Catherine once wrote, "I don't believe in any religion apart from doing the will of God."

She lived her life known as "The Army Mother," and she eventually died from cancer at the age of sixty-one. She set an example for us as a great servant and follower of God.

PRAYER

Dear God, thank You for the plan You have for my life. Show me, like You did for Catherine Booth, what that plan is so that I may glorify You always. Amen.

IRENA SENDLER
Humanitarian (1910–2008)
The Secret Rescuer

God calls us to treat every life as precious, but would you help save a life if you knew you could go to prison or be killed for doing so? Irena Sendler risked her life to save the lives of several thousand Jewish children, all because she believed it was the right thing to do.

Irena grew up in Poland. Her father, who worked as a doctor, died when she was around seven. He had been treating people with typhus, a very contagious disease, and got sick himself. He worked with many Jewish patients, so to thank him, they offered to pay for Irena's education.

During this time, Adolf Hitler, a man who hated the Jews, came to power in Germany. He blamed the Jews for the money problems the country was having. Over time some of this hatred spread to other countries too. Hitler's followers were known as the Nazis. They invaded Poland and took over the city of Warsaw where Irena lived.

The Jews were mistreated in Poland just like they were in Germany. At first, Irena was able to help by offering them food and shelter. But the following year, the Germans forced half a million Jews into a walled neighborhood known as the ghetto.

The Bible says, "Love your neighbor as yourself" (Leviticus 19:18). Love is demonstrated in many ways. For Irena, love meant helping her neighbors no matter the cost. She said later, "I was taught that if you see a person drowning, you must jump into the water to save them, whether you can swim or not."

With her credentials as a social worker, Irena gained access to the ghetto. She began rescuing orphans and other children. An underground resistance group known as Zegota formed, and Irena served as the head of its children's division. With the help of others, she smuggled children out of the ghetto by hiding them in sacks and suitcases, sneaking them through a courthouse, or traveling through sewer pipes and secret passages.

One dangerous route was through a heavily guarded church. The children needed to speak Polish and had to know Catholic prayers. They were also given non-Jewish names for their protection. The children had to memorize their new names so they could repeat them if they were ever stopped and questioned.

Irena inspires us to value human life and to oppose evil at all costs.

As conditions worsened, Irena and her colleagues tried to plead with more parents to release their children to them. Irena said, "Those scenes over whether to give a child away were heart-rending. Sometimes, they wouldn't give me the child. Their first question was, 'What guarantee is there that the child will live?' I said, 'None. I don't even know if I will get out of the ghetto alive today.'" Irena and her helpers lived with astonishing bravery!

With the help of priests and social services officials, the children received false documents and were placed in orphanages and convents in the countryside. Meanwhile, the people from the ghetto were sent to a death camp called Treblinka.

The Nazis eventually arrested Irena. Just before the Nazis took her away, she gave a friend a detailed list of all the names and locations of the Jewish children rescued from the camp. In prison, the Nazis tortured Irena, leaving her with broken legs and feet. But she never gave up any information that would harm the children or her helpers.

Irena was sentenced to death for her crime of helping and hiding Jews. However, she escaped at the last moment with the help of a German guard who had been bribed. When the war ended, Irena tried to reunite the Jewish children with their families. Sadly, most of the parents had died at Treblinka.

Irena's story went untold and forgotten for many years until a group of American high school students came across her name. Once her story was brought to light, Irena was honored for her valor and courage.

She died at the age of ninety-eight.

Irena inspires us to value human life and to oppose evil at all costs.

PRAYER

Dear God, thank You for brave people like Irena Sendler who treasure the lives of others. Help us to put aside fears and do what is right no matter the cost. Amen.

LISE MEITNER
Physicist (1878–1968)
An Amazing Mind

Have you ever thought about the first verse of the Bible: "In the beginning God created the heavens and the earth"? This verse talks about not only the world we see (such as plants, animals, the sun, and the moon) but also the world we don't see (such as cells, atoms, molecules, and matter). God blessed an amazing woman named Lise Meitner with the wisdom and knowledge to look into the wonders of the physical and chemical world.

Lise was born into a wealthy family in Vienna, Austria. Despite their Jewish heritage, they were not religious. Lise's father worked as a lawyer, and her mother was a talented musician. Lise grew up learning math, piano, French, and other subjects. Austrian girls at that time were not allowed to attend school beyond the age of fourteen, so Lise's parents supported her education by providing the best tutors for her.

Eager to study science at the university level, Lise knew that it would be a difficult path since many programs did not accept women. She first earned a credential to be a French teacher. Then she was accepted into the physics program at the University of Vienna, where she became the second woman to receive a PhD in science. Unable to find work as a researcher, Lise taught high school physics and experimented with radioactivity in her free time.

Lise asked a former professor if she could attend his lectures at the University of Berlin in Germany. She spent three decades at the school, studying physics and radioactivity. She also converted to Christianity during that time.

Lise's partner in science was a chemist named Otto Hahn. The two set up a lab in a small carpenter's workshop because she was not allowed to use the chemistry lab. Together, they conducted experiments and published studies. After World War I, she became the first female physics professor in Germany. She and Otto continued to make scientific discoveries.

She wanted her discovery to be used for good, not as a weapon of destruction.

Can you imagine working so hard for many years only to have your job snatched away? When Adolf Hitler and his Nazi party first came to power, many Jews lost their jobs. Lise was fired from her position as a professor, but she was still allowed to continue her research. When Hitler invaded Austria, however, Lise's life was in danger.

At great risk and with no possessions, Lise made her way out of the country. Although she carried a Dutch entrance visa, Lise did not have a German exit visa. At the border, Dutch officials convinced the Germans to let her through. God provided for her safety! She then traveled through the Netherlands and into Sweden, where she continued her scientific research.

Everything on Earth is made of tiny particles called atoms. In various experiments, scientists looked at the center of an atom, known as a nucleus, and watched how this center reacted to other elements. Lise realized that when the nucleus of an atom was hit by a particle of another atom, the nucleus stretched and became two smaller atoms, much like a drop of water splitting into two separate drops. This also created energy. This discovery, known as nuclear fission, rocked the scientific world; the news spread like wildfire. Somehow, Lise did not receive proper credit for her amazing work. In fact, her partner, Otto, who still lived in Germany, ended up winning the Nobel Prize for the discovery with no mention of Lise's contributions.

When the United States invited Lise to help develop the atomic bomb, she said, "I will have nothing to do with a bomb." She wanted her discovery to be used for good, not as a weapon of destruction. Lise once said, "I love physics with all my heart. . . . It is a kind of personal love, as one has for a person to whom one is grateful for many things."

She died at the age of eighty-nine. In 1997 chemical element 109 was named Meitnerium in her honor.

Lise inspires us to look at the world with awe and to use our minds well.

PRAYER

Dear God, I can't help but be amazed at Your wondrous creation. Help me to appreciate all that You have blessed us with. Amen.

ROSA PARKS

Activist (1913–2005)

Courageous Risk-Taker

Would you do the right thing if it meant you could get into trouble? Would you do it if God gave you the courage to do so? Life isn't always easy, especially when we see something that is wrong and know we need to do something that is right. Rosa Parks courageously took a stand against a wrong, and she did it sitting down!

America suffered greatly because of the Civil War; the struggle lasted four years, and many people died. However, freedom for African American slaves emerged as the great victory from the war. Unfortunately, even though African Americans were declared free, people still treated them unfairly. In the South, laws known as Jim Crow laws kept white people and black people separate. This separation, called *segregation*, included separate bathrooms, separate entrances to restaurants, separate drinking fountains, and even separate schools. Even years after the Civil War, people struggled to treat each other equally.

Growing up in the South, Rosa Parks saw segregation firsthand. She knew it was wrong because she believed God loves *all* people. Her grandparents read to her from the Bible almost every day. She later wrote, "Stories of God caring for His people were a comfort. I wanted to trust God to take care of me, too, but sometimes that was hard."

Segregation laws were strictly enforced in Montgomery, Alabama, where Rosa and her husband lived during the 1950s. On public buses, African Americans had to board through the front door to pay the driver, then get off and reenter the bus through the back door to sit in a segregated section in the back. Rosa worked as a seamstress in a department store, and like many people, she used the bus to get to and from work.

One evening in 1955, Rosa boarded a bus to ride home. She sat near the back of the bus as usual. As the bus continued to pick up passengers, the driver noticed that there was no room for a man to sit in the white section. The driver told Rosa and the others sitting near her to either find another seat or stand to free up the seats for the white people. When no one moved, the driver told them again. What would you have done? Would you have moved as the driver ordered or stayed in your seat to protest? The other three passengers didn't want any trouble, so they got up and moved. Rosa did not move. And when the driver asked again, she said no. Rosa took a stand for her right. She deserved a seat on the bus and set an example by standing firm.

"God's peace flooded my soul, and my fear melted away."

Of course, Rosa was afraid. When a black person refused the orders of a white person, bad things often happened. But she later wrote, "I instantly felt God give me the strength to endure whatever would happen next. God's peace flooded my soul, and my fear melted away. All people were equal in the eyes of God, and I was going to live like the free person God created me to be." How courageous!

Police came and arrested Rosa. She was released later that night, but her arrest began an important chain of events. African American leaders in the city organized a bus boycott—they encouraged people to stay off the city buses on the day of Rosa's court trial. Hundreds of people walked to school and work or stayed home in protest. Meanwhile, the judge found Rosa guilty of breaking the law. Rosa made a hard choice to stand up for what was right in God's eyes.

The Montgomery bus boycott lasted 381 days! During that time, Rosa and her husband lost their jobs and moved to Michigan, where Rosa found a job as a secretary for a US congressman.

Over time, the Supreme Court, the highest court in the land, said the Jim Crow laws were illegal. Buses no longer had black and white sections. What an incredible victory!

Rosa lived to the age of ninety-two. She was laid in honor in the Capitol Rotunda in Washington, DC, where fifty thousand people paid their respects to the "Mother of the Civil Rights Movement."

Rosa inspires us to find courage with God's help so we can do what is right.

PRAYER

Dear God, thank You for Rosa's courage and willingness to do hard things. Help me to stand up for what is right, even when it seems difficult. Amen.

LOTTIE MOON
Missionary (1840–1912)
For the Love of Others

Would you go halfway around the world and give up the comforts of home to tell strangers about God's love? Lottie Moon had a heart to share God's love with others, and she went to China to do it!

Lottie grew up in a wealthy family in Virginia. This allowed her to have an education that most girls did not have at that time. She learned Greek, Spanish, French, Latin, and Hebrew and became the first woman in the South to earn a master's degree!

Although she was raised in a Southern Baptist home, Lottie rejected the teachings of the Bible for years. It wasn't until her friends, who had been praying for her, invited her to a revival meeting that she realized that God truly loved her. As she learned more about God, she also wanted to teach, so she became a teacher at a girls' school in Kentucky.

When we follow God, He can use the various events in our lives for His purposes. While in Kentucky, Lottie met some missionaries to China. She started to donate money to the Southern Baptist's Foreign Mission Board to help the Chinese people learn about Jesus.

At that time, the Southern Baptist Church did not allow single women to serve as missionaries. However, one married missionary couple made arrangements for the wife's single sister to join them. When Lottie's own sister, Edmonia, heard that, she got permission from the Mission Board and went to Tengchow in China as a missionary. After a while, Edmonia urged Lottie to come as well.

After hearing a sermon about the need for more missionaries and spending time in prayer, Lottie felt God calling her to China. Despite relatives and others wondering why American women would want to waste their time in China, Lottie left her job, home, and family to join her sister.

The Chinese people often avoided and rejected Lottie, who stood at only four feet three inches. Nevertheless, she learned to speak Chinese, taught at a school for girls, and traveled to various villages to tell people about God's love for them. In time, people came to accept Lottie, and some even believed in Jesus. Lottie faced disease, turmoil, and loneliness, especially after Edmonia needed to return to the United States because of illness. But Lottie had fallen in love with China and wanted the people to know Jesus.

"China is my joy and my delight. It is my home now."

Lottie wrote many letters urging American churches to send more missionaries. She challenged Southern Baptist women to financially support missionaries to China. She suggested that the ladies spend time praying for missions and then take an offering at Christmas. The Lottie Moon Christmas Offering is still an event that happens every year. She also warned any new missionaries coming that they would have "a life of hardship, responsibility, and constant self-denial."

Unfortunately, some of the Chinese people who believed in Jesus faced persecution. Often, their family members beat them for refusing to follow ancient traditions. One time, Lottie traveled to aid Chinese Christians who were under attack. Because the trip was risky for a foreigner and Christian, Lottie dressed as a Chinese official. With courage and confidence that only God could give her, she made it safely to comfort those who had been tortured.

When Lottie returned to the United States at age sixty-three for a visit, friends pleaded with her to retire. Although she was in poor health, she said, "Nothing could make me stay here. China is my joy and my delight. It is my home now."

Several years later, China faced a severe famine. Because the Foreign Mission Board had no money to send, Lottie spent all she had to help her starving neighbors. She even stopped eating so they could eat instead. What sacrificial love! When another missionary discovered Lottie's poor health, she helped Lottie get onto a boat for America. On the way, however, Lottie died at the age of seventy-two.

She once said, "I have never found mission work more enjoyable. . . . I constantly thank God that He has given me work that I love so much."

Lottie inspires us to do all we can to share God's love with others.

PRAYER

Dear God, help me see the needs around me more clearly. Help me to focus on the needs of others more than my own. Amen.

WILMA RUDOLPH
Olympic Athlete (1940–1994)
Determined to Run

Is there someone in your life who has a disability—a physical or mental handicap that limits the person's movements or activity? Perhaps you struggle with a disability yourself and you would like for other people to understand what you go through. This is a story about a girl named Wilma who had a big disability growing up but did not let it stop her from living a full, happy life.

Little Wilma was born in the backwoods of Tennessee in a tiny shack. Because she arrived so early, her family did not think she would survive. Back then, in the 1940s, African Americans did not have access to the best hospitals. And because Wilma's family was poor, that did not help either. It seemed that the tiny baby would have health problems for the rest of her life. In fact, Wilma had many childhood diseases, including polio, scarlet fever, and pneumonia. These left her weak and fragile and even caused one of her legs to be deformed and unusable.

She needed braces on her legs to help her walk. She had to go to physical therapy for years to build up her strength. But Wilma Rudolph was *determined* to one day walk without braces. So, at the age of nine, she took them off and decided she would do everything she could to walk, run, and play like other kids. She trusted God to help her, and she didn't give up. Later in life, she recalled, "My doctors told me I would never walk again. My mother told me I would. I believed my mother."

Wilma came from a very large family. She was one of twenty-two children! She once said this about her giant family: "When you come from a large, wonderful family, there's always a way to achieve your goals."

Amazingly, Wilma began walking, running, playing basketball, and even racing at track meets. At first, she lost every single race. In fact, she ran so slow, people told her to give it up. But Wilma was determined! She kept running track, and finally she won her first race. And you know what? From that point on, she won almost every race she ran.

Wilma used her success to help create more equality in America.

Gaining the attention of college track coaches, Wilma enrolled at Tennessee State. Her coach, Ed Temple, took her under his wing. He was such a good coach, he helped Wilma make it to the Olympics. In 1960, the Olympics were held in Rome, Italy. Wilma shocked the world by winning three gold medals! She was named Female Athlete of the Year. People considered her the fastest woman in the world.

When Wilma returned home to Tennessee, the governor wanted to have a big parade in her honor. At this time, people were often segregated based upon race. Wilma insisted that there be no division between whites and African Americans at the parade, and the governor agreed. Wilma used her success to help create more equality in America. She knew each person had value because they were made in God's image.

Wilma's accomplishments throughout her lifetime inspire us to work hard and never settle because someone tells us we cannot achieve our dreams. Wilma eventually worked as a teacher, a coach, a public speaker, an author, and a sport's commentator. She even got invited to the White House by President John F. Kennedy!

Wilma became an inspiration for people all over the world. Even during times of sickness, segregation (because of the color of her skin), and hardship, she pressed on. One of her famous quotes is "Never underestimate the power of dreams and the influence of the human spirit. We are all the same in this notion. The potential for greatness lives within each of us."

Wilma Rudolph not only believed in the potential for greatness, but she lived it. She passed on a wonderful legacy for her kids, her grandkids, and many generations to come.

PRAYER

Dear God, help me to be like Wilma Rudolph, who did not let her limitations stop her. Give me determination and strength to do what You have called me to do. Thank You for people like Wilma who inspire us all. Amen.

LUCY JANE RIDER MEYER

Social Worker (1849–1922)

Tireless Worker for God

Have you ever felt that you have nothing to contribute to God's work here on earth? Do you know that if you trust Him to use you, God can make amazing things happen? He used Lucy Rider Meyer's restless energy to bless many people throughout the world.

Lucy was born in Vermont and grew up with a wide variety of educational interests. She graduated at age eighteen from a theological seminary in Vermont, attended Oberlin College in Ohio the year it became the first college in the United States to admit women along with men, and went to the Women's Medical School in Philadelphia. She was engaged at this time, and she and her fiancé had planned to serve God together as missionaries once they were married. But he died suddenly during her second year of school.

Returning to Vermont to figure out what God wanted her to do next, Lucy started teaching Sunday school. The Sunday school lessons and Bible quizzes she wrote and published became very popular. When she was twenty-seven, she served as a principal at a Vermont school; the next year, she specialized in science at a technology school in Boston; and at age twenty-nine she studied the Methods of Teaching in Chicago. The following year, she became a college chemistry professor and worked at the school for four years. She later resigned her position so she could work for the Illinois State Sunday School Association.

Lucy merged together her love of school and church, and God started forming a dream. During this time, she married Josiah S. Meyer, a businessman who shared her passion for serving God.

Shortly after getting married, Lucy shared her ideas for a training school with a women's missionary society. The ladies' group liked her ideas, and within a few months, the Chicago Training School for City, Home, and Foreign Missions opened its doors! Money was short, there were no chairs or desks, and often food and necessities were scarce, but they daily prayed for God to bless them—and God did!

Lucy did so many amazing things because she let God direct her passions.

Lucy used her writing skills to publish articles telling about the work of the training school. The school's purpose was to provide training in the Bible, to prepare the ladies for missionary work in other lands, and to encourage missionary work within the cities. As the students served in different parts of the city, various needs of the community were presented to them. Lucy and her husband worked together to meet those needs.

Over time, God used that training school to create hospitals, schools, a rest home, orphanages, and nursing homes. Constantly on the go, Lucy handled administrative duties, helped with housework, taught classes, held interviews, and wrote books, articles, and songs. She gave birth to her son (though she was bedridden for a while) and even completed medical school!

Lucy did so many amazing things because she let God direct her passions. What could this look like in your life? Can you think of what you love and try using it to honor God and help others know Him? Lucy did just that.

As the work continued and the years went by, health issues began to bother her. Lucy and Josiah decided to retire from the school. She had said, "I shall have to give up the work sometime, and why not go while I am young and strong enough to turn my hand at something else?" Even though Josiah wanted her to rest, Lucy continued to write and find various projects to keep her busy.

Eventually Lucy's health problems were too much for her body to endure. She died at age seventy-three. When Josiah and Lucy left the school, over 300 of their students had become missionaries in foreign countries and over 1,500 were working in missions in America.

Lucy inspires us to use our gifts for God's purposes.

PRAYER

Dear God, sometimes I am not sure what You want me to do with my life. But I know as long as I trust You, You will direct me and provide for me, just like You did for Lucy Meyer. Amen.

CLARE OF ASSISI
Italian Saint (1194–1253)
A True Prayer Warrior

How much time do you spend in prayer? Minutes? Hours? Prayer is our way to talk to God. When we pray, we can tell Him about our troubles, we can share with Him how much we love Him, we can ask Him to help and protect people we love, and we can ask for direction for our lives. Clare of Assisi spent much of her life praying because she strongly believed in the importance of prayer.

Chiara Offreduccio (Clare in English) was born over eight hundred years ago in Assisi, Italy. She had all the comforts she could ask for since her family was very wealthy and lived in a palace. Clare knew how to read and write, how to spin yarn, and how to do needlework. And at an early age, she devoted herself to following God. Inspired by her mother's example, Clare felt compelled to help those less fortunate than herself. She often set aside some of her own food in order to share it with the poor and hungry.

When Clare was a teenager, her parents wanted her to marry a rich, young man, but Clare turned down the offer. Instead of wishing for wealth and family, she wanted to follow the example of Francis, whom she had heard preach at one of the churches in the area. Francis, who was about thirteen years older than Clare, was also born into a wealthy family in Assisi. But he came to know Jesus and desired to lead a life of poverty, purity, and obedience. Clare ran away from her home to Francis's Porziuncola Chapel. There, she traded her fine clothes for a simple robe and veil. In place of her jeweled belt, she used a knotted rope to hold up her clothes. She even let Francis cut her long hair. Then, Clare made a promise to dedicate her life to God.

Clare's father and other family members barged into the Benedictine convent where she was staying. They tried to force her to leave, but Clare clung to the chapel altar, saying she wanted to stay and serve only Jesus. Shortly afterward, Clare's sister, Agnes, joined her. Her mother came later, too. As more ladies desired to join Clare, a place was made for the group near a church. Because they chose to live a life of poverty, their group became known as the Poor Ladies of San Damiano. They didn't eat meat, didn't speak most of the time, didn't wear shoes, and spent much time in prayer. By the time Clare was twenty-one, she became the abbess—the head nun—of the convent.

God heard and answered Clare's prayers for protection.

The Poor Ladies relied on the gifts of others to survive. At one point, the pope, the head of the Catholic Church in nearby Rome, tried to convince Clare to abandon such a harsh lifestyle. She replied, "I need to be absolved [freed] from my sins, but I do not wish to be absolved from the obligation of following Jesus Christ."

Clare ministered to those who came to the convent. She washed the feet of nuns and spoke with the popes, cardinals, and bishops who came to see her. On more than one occasion, the prayers of Clare were credited with saving the town from invaders. The Bible tells us that God hears the prayers of His people. God heard and answered Clare's prayers for protection.

Francis and Clare remained close friends and partners in ministry. When Francis neared the end of his life, Clare cared for him. Although she herself was seriously ill for many years, Clare continued to care for other people and to daily live her life for Jesus. She died at the age of fifty-nine.

The Order of St. Clare continues to grow in more than seventy countries around the world. Tens of thousands of women have taken vows and joined the order in hopes of following in Clare's footsteps, serving Jesus.

Clare inspires us to be prayerful and to live a life for Jesus.

PRAYER

Dear God, help me to spend more time talking to You in prayer than I do now. Help me to learn to put the needs of others first instead of only being concerned about me. Amen.

FANNY CROSBY
Composer (1820–1915)
Poet for God

Do you thank God for everything in your life, both the good and the bad? Would you thank God if you were blind? Fanny Crosby could have been bitter about not being able to see, but instead she thanked God through her beautiful poems and songs.

When Fanny was six weeks old, she developed an eye infection. A man pretending to be a doctor treated her with a hot mustard pack over her eyes. Although the infection went away, the hot treatment left her blind. Shortly afterward, Fanny's father died. Her mother worked as a maid to provide for the family.

Fanny was taken care of by her grandmother, who helped Fanny "see" the world around her. The two would go on walks, and her grandmother would describe the things she saw. She would also read the Bible to Fanny and talk to her about praying and having a good relationship with God. Fanny would later write, "My grandmother was more to me than I can ever express by word or pen."

From the start, Fanny never let her blindness get her down. At the age of eight, she wrote one of her first poems:

Oh, what a happy soul I am, although I cannot see!

I am resolved that in this world contented I will be.

How many blessings I enjoy that other people don't,

to weep and sigh because I'm blind I cannot, and I won't!

She had a deep understanding of what it means to be grateful. When she was older she wrote, "It seemed intended by the blessed providence of God that I should be blind all my life, and I thank Him for the dispensation."

Fanny was a gifted poet and had an amazing ability to memorize the things she heard. She knew chapters from the Bible by heart because she would memorize large portions each week. She loved God's words and later wrote, "The Holy Book has nurtured my entire life."

She had a deep understanding of what it means to be grateful.

When Fanny was fourteen, she was accepted into a new school, the New York Institute for the Blind. During her twelve years there as a student, Fanny continued to write poetry. Eventually several newspapers published her work, and later her writings even appeared in two poetry books. She became a teacher at the school, and she taught English and history for eleven years. During that time she met presidents and congressmen. She began writing lyrics for songs as well.

Just before her thirty-eighth birthday, Fanny married a former pupil and fellow teacher at the school. He was an accomplished organist, and the two composed many songs together. Fanny could play the harp, guitar, piano, and other instruments. That same year, Fanny left her teaching position and published her third book of poetry.

Musicians often asked Fanny to write lyrics for their music. Once a musician came to Fanny just minutes before he had to catch a train. He needed words to accompany a song he was to play at a convention. Fanny listened to the tune and immediately wrote one of her most popular hymns, "Safe in the Arms of Jesus."

Fanny often wrote several hymns a day, praying before each one for God's inspiration. She enjoyed writing songs that could be used to share the love of Jesus. Fanny wrote so many hymns that she often signed them with different names so people wouldn't know she had written them. She became known as America's "Hymn Queen." One of her most famous hymns that many people still sing is "Blessed Assurance."

In addition to writing songs, Fanny was involved in missions work. She and her husband lived in a rough part of New York City. They became friends with a popular preacher who ministered nearby. Fanny sometimes counseled those who came to hear him speak. Her approach to telling people about God was always to focus on the joy that comes from accepting God's love and forgiveness.

Fanny continued to write, publishing another book of poetry and two autobiographies. She was ninety-five when she died.

Fanny inspires us to use our talents for God and to thank Him in all situations.

PRAYER

Dear God, help me to develop the skills You have given me, and help me to thank You for the things in life that come my way. Amen.

JEANETTE LI
Evangelist (1899–1968)
Beyond Fairy Tales

Do you know someone who is struggling with sadness or pain or sickness right now? No one hopes for suffering in their life, but some people allow God to use them in the midst of their suffering to show others His love. This is the way Jeanette Li lived. Jeanette was born in South China in 1899. Now, Jeanette's father had hoped for a baby boy to carry on the family name. So, when a daughter was born instead, he chose to raise her like a son and send her to school. This was unheard of!

As a child, Jeanette had a lot of doubts about her father's beliefs. He followed many superstitions, which means he believed in things that were like fairy tales. Jeanette would ask him all kinds of questions about why he believed what he did. Even though she was only a little girl, Jeanette knew that something about her father's beliefs did not make sense.

Sadly, when Jeanette was only six years old, her father passed away. That left Jeanette and her sister to be raised by their mother. Of course, her mother had to work most of the time, so Jeanette spend part of the year living with another family.

At the age of seven, Jeanette grew ill with a very high fever. Her mother hurried to take her to a Chinese doctor, but a relative urged her to take Jeanette to a mission hospital instead. Jeanette's mother was afraid of the mission hospital because of the superstition that the doctors would pluck out children's eyes! But the relative finally convinced her to rush Jeanette to the mission hospital, which was closest.

Fortunately, Jeanette's mother listened to the relative, for it was at the mission hospital that Jeanette not only received treatment for her fever but also heard about God. No one plucked out any eyes! The doctors shared the good news about Jesus with Jeanette, and she believed in Him.

When remembering her time in the hospital, she once wrote this about God: "He used sickness and death to break up the home in which I had been lovingly nestled. But He did not cast me off and forsake me. As the eagle He 'spread forth His wings, caught me up in His wings,' and carried me even to His own Home to become His child."

"In every period of my life, I have found God sufficient for my every need, for my help in every weakness."

Jeanette went on to study at a Christian school for girls and was baptized at the age of ten. Unfortunately, the school closed down a few years later due to a war in China. Jeanette and her mother had no place to go. They tried to return to their relatives but were not accepted because of their Christian faith. Their family members did not like that Jeanette and her mother no longer believed in their traditional superstitions.

It was a custom in China for girls to get married at the age of sixteen, and even though Jeanette wanted to further her studies, she became the wife of a man named Lei Wing Kwan. Together, they had a son and a daughter, but the daughter died as an infant. When her husband went to serve in the military, they grew apart until Jeanette was left alone to support herself and her son.

Even without much money, Jeanette found a way to provide for her son and her sick mother. She somehow found the strength to continue her studies, become a teacher, and eventually go into mission work.

Her heart for God and the Bible took her to Northeast China, to a place called Manchuria, where she lived for fourteen years. There, she started a school, taught the Bible, and feared for her life. At one point, the Manchurian government imprisoned her for her beliefs. During her imprisonment, the guards beat her, neglected to give her food, and forced her to work. Still, she told all the other prisoners about God and her faith in Him!

Jeanette spent the remainder of her life living with her son, Timothy, in Los Angeles, California. She ministered to the Chinese community and wrote her autobiography. In one part of her book she wrote, "In every period of my life, I have found God sufficient for my every need, for my help in every weakness."

Jeanette is a good example of a woman who believed in God more than fairy tales or superstitions. She was a remarkable woman of faith.

PRAYER

Dear God, please help me to trust You even when people around me might not understand who You are. Help me to follow Jeanette's example of faith in You. Amen.

MARY KAY ASH

Executive (1918–2001)

The Cosmetic Queen

The Bible tells us to put God first in our lives, but how should we do this? Do we do this in every area or just when we go to church or pray? Mary Kay Ash made sure to put God first in everything she did in her life.

Mary Kay was born in Texas toward the end of World War I. Her father had tuberculosis, a disease that affects the lungs. Starting at age seven, she often had to care for him on her own since her mother had to work to support the family. She learned how to cook, clean, and serve as a nurse for her dad. If she was ever uncertain, her mother would give her directions and then say, "You can do it, Mary Kay. You can do it."

When Mary Kay got married, she helped earn money by selling books door-to-door. At the age of twenty-one, she worked for Stanley Home Products. But instead of selling from a store or door-to-door, she sold their products at home parties. Mary Kay's natural ability to sell a product led her to a lot of success. After several years, she was hired by World Gifts. For more than a decade, Mary Kay held the position of salesperson. Meanwhile, newer and less experienced employees, all of whom were men, moved up in the ranks through promotions. She had even trained many of these men. Now they made more money and earned more praise than Mary Kay!

Mary Kay didn't like how unfair companies were to women. But what could she do? She realized that the only way to achieve success was to start a company of her own. With the knowledge she had gained from her past sales jobs, Mary Kay took the $5,000 she had in savings, spent $500 of it to buy a skin lotion recipe from a friend's father, and opened a store in Dallas with the help of her son. They used the home party model Mary Kay had learned from Stanley Home Products: The salesperson (or consultant, as Mary Kay called them) would recruit a friend to host a party. The hostess would invite friends to a party at her home. The consultant would demonstrate products and let guests try them. In addition to selling products, the consultant would try to get other guests to host their own parties.

"My priorities have always been God first, family second, career third."

Even though they started with only five products to sell, the company was immediately successful. After two years, it had sold about $1 million in products! The driving force behind this success was Mary Kay herself. She was a gifted salesperson with a mind for business. She later said, "My priorities have always been God first, family second, career third. I have found that when I put my life in this order, everything seems to work out. God was my first priority early in my career when I was struggling to make ends meet. Through failures and success I have experienced since then, my faith has remained unchecked." How inspiring!

Mary Kay put her beliefs into action by equipping women to be successful in their careers. Her consultants could set their own hours, working as much or as little as they liked. This allowed them to put God and family before career in their lives. Consultants also earned extra pay for recruiting new consultants to join the company. They were rewarded for their sales, with incentives from free products to a pink Cadillac car! Today, more than 1.6 million salespeople work for

Mary Kay, Inc. The company sells more than $2.2 billion in products each year. Consultants operate in almost forty different countries.

Mary Kay led the company with enthusiasm and encouragement. She always remembered her mother telling her, "You can do it."

She died at age eighty-three.

Mary Kay inspires us to put God first always and to be grateful for the blessings in our lives.

PRAYER

Dear God, sometimes I get so busy that I forget to put You first. Help me to remember that I can do nothing without You and that I can always trust in You. Amen.

AMY CARMICHAEL
Missionary (1867–1951)
Determined to Serve

Have you ever really wanted to do something, but obstacles kept getting in your way? It is hard to wait. Amy Carmichael wanted to serve God, but He kept her waiting because He had a perfect plan for her.

Amy Carmichael was born to a wealthy family in Ireland. Both parents were devout Christians, and Amy and her six younger siblings were raised with a deep faith in God. Once, when Amy was young, her mother told her that God answers prayer. So Amy prayed that God would give her blue eyes instead of her brown eyes. When she woke up the next morning, she ran to the mirror and was very disappointed that God did not answer her prayer. When she told her mother, her mother said that God *did* answer—the answer was no.

Life changed suddenly when the family business starting failing. Amy's father was so worried that he became sick and died. Amy had to leave school to help her mother care for her brothers and sisters.

As a young woman, Amy felt a strong desire to care for people in need and to tell them about Jesus. She and a local pastor would go into the poor areas of the city to hand out food and pamphlets that taught about God's love. Amy was especially touched by the "shawlies," young girls who worked in the factories and covered their heads with their shawls because they couldn't afford hats. Amy began Bible studies and prayer meetings for these girls. Soon, so many were attending that Amy used donations to purchase a building.

Amy then followed God's call to England, where she ministered in another urban slum. Eventually, health problems forced her to stay at the home of a family friend. During that time, she was inspired by a talk given by the well-known missionary to China, Hudson Taylor. Amy's health, however, kept her from the mission field. She had a condition that affected her nerves, causing her to stay in bed for weeks at a time. She later spent some time as a missionary in Japan, but her poor health once again halted her work.

It is easy to get discouraged when you are unable to do what you think God is calling you to do. Why wasn't God allowing Amy to serve Him? She would pray and seek His direction, and she felt that God was telling to her to go, but no missionary group wanted her. So she kept praying.

> *"The best training is to learn to accept everything as it comes, as from Him whom our soul loves."*

Finally, friends invited her to join their group in India. When she arrived, Amy found missionaries doing little to minister to the Indian people. She soon accompanied a pastor to a needier area. Working hard, she learned the local language and customs.

Many girls in India at that time were unwanted by their parents and sold to the Indian temples. Amy heard that these girls were treated badly, but she needed proof. So she darkened her skin and put on an Indian dress called a sari so she could sneak into the temple. Now she realized why God had given her brown eyes. If she had blue eyes, she would have quickly been discovered. Sadly, Amy learned that the rumors were true—these poor girls received horrible treatment.

It wasn't long before Amy rescued her first temple girl. In time, many more would follow. Amy, who knew God's plan for her didn't include a husband or children of her own, was soon "Mother"—or *Amma* in the local language—to a family of more than fifty! When girls showed up at her door, Amy knew she could be charged with kidnapping. However, she also knew that if she turned girls away, they would face terrible punishment or even death.

In time, Amy's illness became worse. She took a bad fall, injuring her back and hip. Nevertheless, Amy continued her beloved missionary work from her bedroom and wrote several books. She once wrote, "The best training is to learn to accept everything as it comes, as from Him whom our soul loves."

She died at age eighty-three.

Amy inspires us to trust God to show us where we are to serve Him, even if it takes a long time.

PRAYER

Dear God, I am not always good at waiting, but sometimes You ask me to wait and to trust You. Help me to be determined, like Amy, to wait until You lead the way. Amen.

CLARA BARTON
Nurse (1821–1912)
Kindhearted Caregiver

Have you ever volunteered at your school or church? Maybe they needed help with cleanup or serving people at an event. Volunteering is one way followers of Jesus can demonstrate God's love for others. Clara Barton showed God's love when she eagerly helped wounded soldiers and others who needed emergency help.

Clara Barton, the youngest of five children, was born in Massachusetts on Christmas Day. As a teenager, she helped care for her brother for two years after he had a serious head injury, an experience that may have planted the seeds of nursing in her. Although Clara was very shy, she became a teacher at the age of eighteen, founded a school for the children of the workers in her brother's mill, and later moved to New Jersey, where she started another school. She resigned after two years when the school board hired a man to run the school and paid him twice her salary! Clara then moved to Washington, DC, where she became the first female recording clerk in the US patent office. There, she earned the same salary as her male coworkers.

When the Civil War broke out, Clara was thirty-nine years old. When wounded soldiers were brought into the capital, she immediately came to their aid. She organized the collection of supplies and gave them comfort through prayer and personal help. She even read to them and wrote letters for them to send to loved ones.

Clara realized that the greatest need for help was at the battlefields, so she sought permission to go where the war was being fought. Such a thing was unheard of for an unmarried woman at the time, but Clara persisted. Finally, permission came. She quit her job at the patent office so she could support Union troops. She brought supplies to needy soldiers in several states. This put her near the frontlines of every major battle in Maryland, Virginia, and South Carolina. Risking her own life, Clara tended to wounded soldiers, who called her the "angel of the battlefield." Even though she had no formal training as a nurse, Clara became head nurse for a unit of soldiers. Her roles included nurse, cook, scribe, counselor, and prayer partner as she helped meet the many needs of the injured soldiers. What a comfort she must have been to those men who had no family nearby!

The American Association of the Red Cross was formed with Clara as its first president.

She once wrote, "I may be compelled to face danger, but never fear it, and while our soldiers can stand and fight, I can stand and feed and nurse them."

Beyond the battlefield, Clara continued her mission of care. She helped former slaves transition to living in freedom. She established an office to help reunite soldiers with their families. For four years, Clara and her team worked to answer sixty-three thousand letters. They were able to identify twenty-two thousand missing men. Even President Lincoln urged people to write to Clara for help identifying missing soldiers. In Georgia, Clara created a cemetery near a former prison. There, she identified the graves of thirteen thousand war prisoners. Clara also spoke before Congress about her experiences in the war.

The stress and troubles of war can take a toll on people, so when the Civil War ended, Clara traveled to Europe to get some much-needed rest.

There, she learned of a new disaster relief group founded in Switzerland, the International Red Cross. During the Franco-Prussian War, Clara served with the Red Cross in France. She distributed supplies to the needy and created workrooms where they could make new clothes. Although she wasn't an official member of the Red Cross, Clara made herself a cross out of red ribbon to wear and went where she was needed.

Clara was eager to create an American branch of the Red Cross. She wrote pamphlets, gave lectures, and even met with President Hayes. Clara's determination paid off. The American Association of the Red Cross was formed with Clara as its first president. She worked well into her eighties helping people through floods, famines, hurricanes, fires, and wars. During that time, Clara also supported women's right to vote.

She died at her home in Maryland at the age of ninety-one.

Clara inspires us to think of others first when there is an immediate need.

PRAYER

Dear God, help me to be willing to give up my time to help others, because in doing this, I reflect Your love. Amen.

SOJOURNER TRUTH
Abolitionist (1797–1883)
Fearless Speaker

Do you believe God can change lives? Do you believe He can take someone who has been mistreated for many, many years and turn that person into a bold speaker for those who cannot speak for themselves? Sojourner Truth had a very harsh young life, but God helped her to fearlessly speak out for the rights of all.

The United States was barely twenty years old when Sojourner—whose birth name was Isabella—was born. She grew up as a slave in a Dutch-speaking community in New York. When her owner died, she was separated from her family and sold to an English-speaking master. She was only nine years old. Because she could not understand the language, she often received beatings for not following instructions.

Sojourner knew no other life than working hard and being mistreated. How would you feel if your life went from one hopeless situation to the next? Where could you turn to for comfort, especially if you had no family around? Sojourner remembered her mother telling her that she could find God in the stars, so when Sojourner found herself alone, she would talk to God and find comfort.

When Sojourner had grown up and had several children, the state of New York set up a law to stop slavery. But Sojourner's master was a trickster. He told her that he would release her a year early but only if she behaved. Sojourner's owner lied. He did not set her free. Sojourner sensed God telling her to leave, so she took her baby daughter and walked away. A nearby family, the Van Wageners, took her in. They did not support slavery. Sojourner learned a lot about the Bible and God's love from this kind couple.

Sojourner soon learned that her son had been sold to an owner in the South. This was against the law in New York, but her old owner didn't care. Sojourner boldly took her case to court—and won! God helped her to get her son back.

Sojourner faced confrontation without showing any fear.

With her two small children, Sojourner moved to New York City. She worked as a housekeeper for two different preachers. One day she had a strong vision telling her to go about the country and tell people about her life as a slave. She felt God calling her to share the truth about His love. It was at this time that she changed her name from Isabella Baumfree to Sojourner Truth. A *sojourner* is a traveler who stays in a place for a short time. And the last name of Truth represented her message to all those who would listen.

Sojourner was six feet tall and had a magnetic personality and a commanding voice. She preached the message of God's goodness in churches, at camp meetings, and on street corners. During this time, she also became an outspoken abolitionist—a person who is opposed to slavery. Sojourner faced confrontation without showing any fear. As her reputation grew, she traveled throughout the country. She spoke to large crowds and sold copies of her book, *The Narrative of Sojourner Truth*. Because she never learned to read or write, she dictated the words in the book to a friend. In time, she also spoke about giving women the right to vote.

Sojourner once said, "Children, who made your skin white? Was it not God? Who made mine black? Was it not the same God? Am I to blame, therefore, because my skin is black? . . . Does not God love the colored children as well as white children? And did not the same Savior die to save the one as well as the other?" Sojourner spoke beautiful, true words.

Sojourner's boldness led her to support black troops in the war, to eventually meet President Abraham Lincoln, and even to help former slaves resettle. Her final words were "Be a follower of the Lord Jesus." She modeled this well her whole life.

PRAYER

Dear God, help me not to be afraid to speak out when I see things that are wrong. Help me to be brave like Sojourner Truth—willing to share Your truth so that lives can be changed for good. Amen.

SOPHIA JEX-BLAKE

Doctor (1840–1912)

Persistent to the End

Imagine that you dreamed about going to a particular city, but a mountain stood in your way. There is no road or trail. Would you have the courage to strike out on your own in order to follow your dream? Sophia Jex-Blake wanted to be a doctor, but she had to create her own path because she was a woman.

Sophia grew up in a wealthy and religious family in England. As a young girl during a time when well-to-do young ladies were expected to marry, raise a family, and take care of the household, Sophia wanted to go to college. At first her parents said no, but in the end they gave in. She got a teaching degree from Queen's College because teaching was one of the few acceptable positions for women at that time. She was a bright student and a gifted speaker.

After college, Sophia traveled to Germany to teach and to study the country's educational system. Next, she traveled to the United States. There, she met a female doctor named Lucy Sewell, who had fought hard for education and social changes in America. Sophia spent some time as her assistant at a hospital for women.

Inspired by this experience, Sophia applied to Harvard University in the United States to study medicine. The school rejected her, claiming, "There is no provision for the education of women in any department of this university." Sophia was accepted into a women's medical school in New York, but she had to return to England when her father died.

Never one to give up easily, Sophia applied to Edinburgh University in Scotland. Her application caused debate among the leaders of the school. At first, they accepted Sophia. Then, she was told they could not make the changes needed in order to accommodate just one female student. Instead of feeling discouraged, Sophia challenged herself to find more students! She ran ads in a Scottish newspaper looking for another woman to join her, and six other women applied to the medical school with Sophia. The "Edinburgh Seven" all passed the entrance exam and began their studies.

Sophia continued to push for women's right to medical education.

However, the women did not have an easy time at Edinburgh University. They had to pay higher fees than male students, and some professors refused to allow them into their classes. After a year, a riot broke out on campus over the female students. More than two hundred people formed a mob and threw mud and garbage at the women as they were on their way to take an exam. The women eventually made it inside. The riot brought a lot of attention to the female students, and many people felt sympathy for them. Wanting to avoid any further trouble, the university refused to allow the women to graduate.

Sophia continued to push for women's right to medical education. She helped establish the London School of Medicine for Women and helped get the Medical Act passed, which allowed women to become licensed in medicine. Sophia finally earned her medical degree in Switzerland, and many of the Edinburgh seven also went to other countries for theirs. When laws changed in the United Kingdom, Sophia became licensed in Dublin, Ireland. She returned to Edinburgh, where she became Scotland's first female doctor. What an achievement! She also founded a school of medicine and a hospital there, both of which catered to women.

Once women had the right to education and medical degrees, Sophia continued fighting for women's rights. During her lifetime, she wrote many medical texts and even some articles about her faith in God. Sophia once wrote to her mother, "I always get greatly interested in a discussion about the Bible—people seem to me often so hopelessly superstitious and illogical about it, and so to miss its truest, most blessed meaning."

She passed away at the age of seventy-one after a series of heart attacks.

Sophia inspires us to trust God to help us achieve His purposes for us.

PRAYER

Dear God, help me to have the courage, like Sophia, to go in the direction You call me to go, even if obstacles seem to block my way. Help me to trust in Your faithfulness. Amen.

"Common sense is seeing things as they are; and doing things as they ought to be."

"Never give up, fo_ _ just the place a_ that the tide will

"Any mind that is capable of a real sorr_ is capable of good."

"It's a matter of taking _e weak against the _mething the best p_ have always done.'

"Women are the _ _rchitects of so_

_nost mothers _ _e philosophers

"So subtle is the at_ of opinion that it _ make itself felt

"We never _ how we lov_ we try to u_

"I did not wr_ (Uncle Tom's _ God wrote I merely _ his _

he water of th is the calme_ _e the deepest

HARRIET BEECHER STOWE
Author (1811–1896)
Gifted Wordsmith

What would you do if people treated your neighbor poorly? Would you do something to help him or her? The Bible tells us we are to love our neighbor and to treat others as we would want to be treated. Harriet Beecher Stowe used her words to help people realize the horrible nature of slavery.

Harriet was born into a large family in Connecticut. Her father, a well-known minister, strongly opposed slavery, and he taught his children to value the lives of all humans. Education was important in the household, and Harriet's older sister, Catharine, started her own school, which Harriet attended. When the family moved to Cincinnati, Ohio, Catharine started another school where Harriet was a teacher.

While in Cincinnati, Harriet began writing stories, articles, and even a textbook. She attended a writers' group and eventually married one of the members, Calvin Stowe, a seminary professor. She also became more familiar with the truth about slavery—that owning people and abusing them is a wicked practice and a sin in God's eyes. The Ohio River separated Cincinnati from the slave state of Kentucky, so sometimes slaves escaped by crossing the river. Once they had safely crossed, they would tell about their experiences. Harriet listened to their stories and visited a plantation in Kentucky. She also read the writings of those who opposed slavery.

Harriet, Calvin, and their children moved to Maine about fourteen years after they married so Calvin could work as a professor at Bowdoin

College. During that time, Harriet's eighteen-month-old son died. Congress also passed the Fugitive Slave Act that required escaped slaves in both free and slave states to be returned to their owners. This law, combined with the experiences of helping a fugitive slave and losing her child, inspired Harriet to write a long, fictional account of slavery. In her writing, she made the readers see that slaves were human beings with feelings, not just pieces of property.

At first, the story was published in several parts in an antislavery newspaper. Then it was published as a book, *Uncle Tom's Cabin*. The book immediately became popular, selling ten thousand copies in one week, three hundred thousand copies in its first year, and two million copies worldwide within five years! In the South, however, the book was hated. Anyone caught reading or even owning it could face persecution.

The strong message in Harriet's book convinced readers that slavery is wrong.

The novel tells the tale of various slaves and their trials. It also looks at the different views of those who are against slavery, those who accept it, and those who keep it working. The main character, Tom, is a slave and a devout Christian. Often mistreated, he is eventually beaten to death by a cruel master. His sacrifice serves as a powerful reminder of the evils of slavery.

The strong message in Harriet's book convinced readers that slavery is wrong. Harriet understood that God wants people to show kindness to all people, especially to those who are treated unfairly. People around the world were moved by the way the novel made slavery feel personal. The slaves in the story had families, dreams, and beliefs that made the issue of slavery come to life for readers.

Uncle Tom's Cabin was translated into many languages and even turned into a popular stage production. After the success of *Uncle Tom's Cabin*, Harriet continued to write books and newspaper articles. She vacationed in Florida, where she and one of her sons established a plantation to hire former slaves and give them a better life.

She died at the age of eighty-five.

Harriet inspires us to use the gifts God has given us to help those who cannot help themselves.

PRAYER

Dear God, help me to see the needs of others, and then show me how to help them. Amen.

MADELEINE L'ENGLE
Author (1918–2007)
Called to Write

Have you ever thought of being a writer? Have you looked at the cover of a book and thought how nice it would be to one day see your name on a book too? From a young age, Madeleine L'Engle wanted to be a published writer, and she used much of her writing to honor God.

Madeleine was born in New York City around the end of World War I. Her father had been an overseas reporter in the army, and her mother was a gifted pianist. While her parents loved having their little girl, their busy schedules did not always have room for her. So Madeleine did what she liked best: she read and wrote and created her own imaginary worlds. She claimed that she had "been a writer ever since [she] could hold a pencil."

When Madeleine was in fifth grade, she won a poetry competition. One of her teachers, however, didn't believe Madeleine could write a prize-winning poem. Madeleine's mother came to her rescue, bringing an armload of her stories as proof of her creative ability.

When she was twelve, Madeleine and her family moved to Europe for a few years, and she attended a boarding school in Switzerland. She continued at a boarding school in South Carolina when they returned to the United States. Tragedy struck, however, when Madeleine was seventeen. Her father died after years of health problems caused by mustard gas exposure during World War I.

To pursue her dream of becoming an author, Madeleine earned an English degree from Smith College. She published her first novel, *The Small Rain*, a few years later. The book was well-received, but her second novel, *Ilsa*, was not as successful. Madeleine also worked as a writer and actress in theater during this time. While working on a production, she met actor Hugh Franklin. The two married and eventually had three children.

Madeleine's first published children's book was *And Both Were Young*. She continued to write but had trouble getting some of her books published. She and her husband ran a general store in Connecticut to earn a living. After receiving yet another rejection letter on her fortieth birthday, Madeleine almost gave up writing. However, she could not shake the need to write, especially since she knew her ability to write was a gift given to her by God.

> *She knew her ability to write was a gift given to her by God.*

Writing a young adult book called *Meet the Austins* helped put her back on track. The book drew from her experiences of losing her father and adopting a child. Readers loved its honesty. At the same time, she was working on her most famous work, *A Wrinkle in Time.*

A Wrinkle in Time was rejected around thirty times before a publisher finally accepted it. The book received great acclaim and to date has sold over eight million copies! It tells of an epic cosmic battle against evil as children travel through time. The unusual story drew upon Madeleine's interest in science and religion. It won the highest honor in children's literature, the John Newbery Medal. Madeleine followed it up with three sequels, which were also popular.

Despite the great success of the series, some readers did not approve of the content. Accusations of anti-Christian messages caused the book to be banned in many places. This reaction puzzled Madeleine, who was a Christian and frequently included themes from the Bible in her books. About her faith she wrote, "I have been brought up to believe that the Gospel is to be spread, it is to be shared—not kept for those who already have it. Well, 'Christian novels' reach Christians. They don't reach out . . . I am not a 'Christian writer.' I am a writer who is a Christian."

In her lifetime, Madeleine wrote over sixty books that included essays, poetry, and memoirs. She died at the age of eighty-eight.

Madeleine inspires us to develop the skills God has given us and to use them to give Him glory.

PRAYER

Dear God, You have a purpose for my life. Help me to appreciate the gifts You have given me to fulfill that purpose. Amen.

MADAM C. J. WALKER
Businesswoman (1867–1919)
Inventor of Solutions

Have you ever come up with one of your own inventions? Perhaps you created a new idea for a science fair display at school. Some people are really talented when it comes to new ideas or solutions to problems.

There once was a girl by the name of Sarah who invented a solution to a problem she had. She was born in 1867 to parents who lived on a plantation. They had been slaves before the Civil War and had worked extremely hard most of their lives.

When she was only fourteen years old, Sarah married Moses McWilliams. Sadly, her husband died two years later, leaving Sarah with a baby girl to raise. Sarah went to live with her brothers, who worked in a barber shop. She worked in their shop for $1.50 per day and sent her daughter to school.

In her mid-twenties, Sarah developed a skin condition that caused her hair to start falling out. Of course, she was not happy about it. But instead of doing nothing, she decided to create her own hair products to solve the problem!

Back in the 1800s, there weren't many hair products to choose from. So, she experimented with different home treatments and eventually came up with her own hair cream. She traveled around the United States selling "Madam Walker's Wonderful Hair Grower." She also gave demonstrations on how her special formula worked.

You might be wondering why she named her product Madam Walker's Wonderful Hair Grower. Who was Madam Walker? Well, Sarah had married a man named Charles Joseph Walker, a newspaper worker. Together, they came up with the name, and Sarah thought it sounded professional. So, she went by the name Madam C. J. Walker from that point on. Eventually, she created Madam C. J. Laboratories and began manufacturing her hair products; she started using machines to make her products in large quantities. This helped Madam C. J. make many bottles of her Wonderful Hair Grower at one time instead of making them one by one.

The hair cream was especially helpful to African American women, and Madam C. J. showed them how to use the cream along with heated brushes to style their hair. She also began to train other women to sell her beauty items. She opened a beauty school and taught the girls all about her products. They became known as the "Walker Girls" and spread Madam C. J.'s message about "cleanliness and loveliness." There is no doubt that Madam C. J. had a God-given talent for business.

There is no doubt that Madam C. J. had a God-given talent for business.

Over time, her cosmetic company grew by leaps and bounds. In fact, Madam C. J. Walker was one of the first American women to become a millionaire! Not only did she make a lot of money, but she also gave a lot of it away. She had a deep faith in God and wanted to help other people. One of the ways she gave back to her community was by helping to fund the YMCA in Indianapolis. Perhaps you have heard of the YMCA. It is a club where people go to exercise and enjoy fun activities. The letters *Y-M-C-A* stand for the Young Men's Christian Association. But today, it is enjoyed by both boys and girls of all ages.

As Madam C. J.'s Laboratory continued to supply the hair products and the Walker Girls continued to spread her message, Madam C. J. traveled to Latin America and throughout the Caribbean, where she sold her products and trained women.

Finally, Madam C. J. returned to the United States and settled down in Harlem, New York. She continued to donate money to many causes and charities, especially those that helped African Americans. She generously supported not only education but also the elderly and the poor.

We can learn so much from Madam C. J.'s example of hard work and generosity. She diligently worked to solve a big problem, and with her earnings, she solved even more problems in the world.

PRAYER

Dear God, thank You for Madam C. J. Walker's example. She was a remarkable woman who did not let her problems keep her down. Help me to have the strength to work hard to find solutions to my problems. And help me to use those solutions to help others. Amen.

BESSIE COLEMAN
Aviator (1892–1926)
Flying above Limitations

Have you ever flown in an airplane? What was it like? Perhaps you felt a little scared when the plane took off. Maybe you felt a few bumps as the airplane flew through some clouds. Whatever your experience, it was probably much different than Bessie's first flying adventure.

Bessie Coleman was born in Texas in 1892. Her father—who was both African American and Native American—worked as a sharecropper, which meant he was allowed to grow crops on someone else's land and make money selling what he grew. Her mother was African American. Because they lived during the time when African Americans were treated unfairly, the family struggled. Bessie's father believed that if they moved away from Texas and went to Oklahoma, things would be different. Bessie's mother did not agree. She wanted to stay in Texas. Sadly, when Bessie was only nine years old, her father left the family and went to Oklahoma by himself.

With her older brothers grown and gone, Bessie took care of her sisters while her mother worked as a maid. Bessie loved to read and was very good at math. Even though she had many responsibilities at home, she tried to make time to learn.

During harvest, when the cotton crops were finished growing and ready to be picked, Bessie and her sisters had to help in the fields. It was hard work out in the hot sun, and Bessie had to miss school and church because of it. It was a really big job, so the whole family had to pitch in to help.

Bessie finally finished all eight grades of school—the total number of grades that were offered back then. After that, she saved every penny so she could go to college. It took her four years to save and only one semester to spend it! Poor Bessie did not have enough money to finish. So, she went to live with one of her brothers and his wife in Chicago, where she worked as a manicurist. Even though she was grateful for the job, she knew she wanted to do something else in life.

When talking about her future goals with her brother, he mentioned that women in France could fly planes. Well, that did it! Bessie made up her mind, right then and there, to become the very first female African American pilot. The problem was, she didn't have anyone to teach her how to fly an airplane.

> *Bessie made up her mind . . . to become the very first female African American pilot.*

While she was still working as a manicurist, she met a man by the name of Robert Abbott. When she told Robert about her dream of becoming a pilot, he told her about an aviation school in France. Oh, how Bessie wanted to go to aviation school and learn to fly a plane!

Fortunately for Bessie, Robert and several other friends put their money together and helped her take a ship all the way to France. After learning how to fly an airplane and put on air shows, Bessie returned to the United States. She put on air shows in New York, Illinois, Tennessee, and Texas.

One of Bessie's big goals was to buy her own airplane. To hurry up the process, she opened a beauty shop, gave lectures, and even did parachute jumping! Can you imagine that? She was a very brave young lady indeed.

After years of performing air shows and saving her money, Bessie was finally able to buy her own airplane. Every time she did an air show, she made sure all viewers were allowed to enter through the same gate. Because she was African American, she knew how it felt to be treated differently. During her air shows, she did not want to see any segregation, or separation, of people.

When Bessie died, more than five thousand people came to her funeral to honor the woman who overcame many obstacles to become the first female African American pilot. Let Bessie's life remind you that trusting God and working hard can help you to accomplish your goals.

PRAYER

Dear God, please help me to work hard in life to accomplish the goals You have for me. Thank You for people like Bessie who showed courage and bravery. Help me to be brave and courageous as well. Amen.

KAYLA MUELLER
Aid Worker (1988–2015)
Modern-Day Martyr

Do you know what a martyr is? A martyr is someone who is put to death for refusing to deny having faith in Jesus. We often think of martyrs from a long time ago when people were first starting to learn about and follow Jesus. But there are martyrs today because people who trust in Jesus are mistreated all over the world. Kayla Mueller was a modern-day martyr who died because she loved Jesus.

Kayla was born in Arizona. While in high school she became interested in protecting the rights of others, especially in areas around the world where people didn't have the same privileges she did. She knew that when people are denied even basic rights, suffering often occurs. She wrote, "For as long as I live, I will not let this suffering be normal."

She joined the Save Darfur Coalition—a group that tried to help the people being mistreated in Sudan in northern Africa—and volunteered with organizations such as AmeriCorps, Youth Count, and Big Brothers Big Sisters. In her senior year of high school, Kayla received a Gold Presidential Volunteer Service Award.

After graduating from college, Kayla went to India to work at an orphanage. She also volunteered in Israel and the West Bank, teaching school and providing aid. Back in the United States, Kayla worked at a clinic and a women's shelter. By her mid-twenties, Kayla had done more good for others than many people do in a lifetime. She followed Jesus' example to help those in need.

Next, Kayla joined the humanitarian group Support to Life in Turkey. A war in the nearby country of Syria caused many to flee, so her group was there to help people who were escaping. Kayla joined a friend for what was to be a quick trip to Aleppo in Syria to repair equipment in a hospital. She knew the trip could be dangerous, but she courageously went anyway.

The job took longer than expected, and the two had to stay overnight at the hospital. On the way back to Turkey the next day, their car was stopped by a group of dangerous people. The passengers, including Kayla, were taken captive.

She would not deny Jesus, no matter what.

Eventually all were released, except for Kayla. They thought she was a spy, and they felt they could get a cash payment for her release. She spent eighteen months in different prisons. At times, Kayla was alone and completely isolated for weeks. Other times, Kayla suffered greatly through beatings, torture, and verbal abuse.

Fellow captives who were later released spoke of Kayla's strength and faith. Once, her captors paraded her in front of other hostages to announce that she had rejected her faith in Jesus. Facing punishment, she declared, "No, I have not." She would not deny Jesus, no matter what. At one point, two young girls discovered a way to escape. They asked Kayla to go with them, but she refused. She knew if she accompanied them, the captors would work hard to hunt them down. Without her, the girls had a better chance of escaping. How brave!

During Kayla's imprisonment, her captors sent a video message to Kayla's parents. At one point, she sent a letter to them. The US government attempted a rescue, but the rescue team arrived just days after Kayla and other captives had been moved. Meanwhile, the captors began killing hostages. Kayla's parents worked frantically to arrange for their daughter's ransom.

Kayla once wrote, "I will always seek God. . . . Some people find God in nature. Some people find God in love; I find God in suffering. I've known for some time what my life's work is, using my hands as tools to relieve suffering."

Tragically, word came that Kayla had been killed in a bombing raid during the war. After a few days, people on the ground confirmed that Kayla had died. Despite their sorrow, Kayla's family said, "We are so proud of the person Kayla was and the work that she did while she was here with us. She lived with purpose, and we will work every day to honor her legacy."

She died at the young age of twenty-six.

Kayla inspires us to always help others, no matter the cost.

PRAYER

Dear God, Kayla was an example of being brave for You. Thank You that wherever I am, You are there to give me strength. Amen.

SUSAN B. ANTHONY

Activist (1820–1906)

Dedicated to the Cause

Many cultures don't treat women with enough respect, but did you know that the Bible says Jesus first appeared to a woman after His resurrection? God values woman and men equally, and He let them both play important roles throughout history. During a time when women were not treated fairly in the United States, Susan B. Anthony fought hard for women's rights.

Susan was born in Massachusetts to a Quaker family. Quakers believed the Bible, which says that God created men and women in His image—this means both men and women are valuable to God. Quakers taught that God created everyone equally and that everyone should be treated the same. This was unusual because in that time period, women could not vote or hold any government positions, a wife could not own property, and a woman could not sue another person in court.

Because her father valued education, Susan learned to read and write at age three, attended good schools, and went on to become a teacher at a Quaker seminary. Susan's parents and her siblings helped shape her into an activist—a person who is passionate about a particular cause or causes. Many of her father's close friends, including former slave Frederick Douglass, opposed slavery. Her mother and sister attended the first Women's Rights Convention in the United States.

Even though people thought it was improper for a woman to give public speeches, Susan began to speak out against slavery. Her frustration in being denied the chance to speak about important issues because she was a woman inspired her to begin working for equal rights for women.

While attending an antislavery meeting, Susan met Elizabeth Cady Stanton. Together, they began working for women's suffrage, or the right to vote. They traveled the country and spoke about women's voting and property rights, as well as antislavery issues.

Susan risked being arrested for boldly speaking out. However, many people liked her ideas and followed her strong leadership. Other people disliked her and her ideas completely. After the Civil War ended, Susan and Elizabeth concentrated on women's rights. They formed the American Equal Rights Association and founded the newspaper *The Revolution*. Through the newspaper and her speaking engagements, Susan spread the idea of equality for women.

She wanted people to work together to create better laws that treated people equally.

At first, people who wanted voting rights for African Americans worked with those who wanted voting rights for women. But when the Fifteenth Amendment, which gave African American men the right to vote, was ratified, Susan and others opposed it because it didn't include women. That caused disagreements between activists.

Susan knew that the fight for women's rights needed the support of many people. She wanted people to work together to create better laws that treated people equally. She faithfully depended on God to give her strength every day. She said, "I pray every single moment of my life; not on my knees but with my work. My prayer is to lift women to equality with men. Work and worship are one with me."

Susan's views on women's rights drove her to vote in a presidential election—even though she wasn't allowed to. When she was arrested, more people paid attention to her cause. For years, she traveled the country. She even met with President Theodore Roosevelt to try to get his support for women's right to vote. Susan continued to serve as the president of her suffrage association until she was eighty years old. During that time, she traveled to other countries to speak about equal rights for men and women. She also wrote several books and papers on the issue of women's suffrage.

Susan died at the age of eighty-six. The Nineteenth Amendment, which gave women the right to vote, passed fourteen years later, in 1920. Even though Susan didn't live to see this incredible law pass, her legacy lived on when the government engraved her image on the US dollar coin.

Susan B. Anthony inspires us to stand up for what is right and live boldly to accomplish our goals.

PRAYER

Dear God, You created men and women in Your image. Help us to value others through Your eyes, and help us to treat others with fairness and love. Amen.

JENNY LIND
Singer (1820–1887)
A God-Given Talent

Do you know that God brings opportunities to us when we least expect them? It could be a chance to make a new friend or to learn a new skill. We may not think these opportunities come from God, but they do. God gave a girl named Jenny Lind a beautiful singing voice.

Jenny was born in Sweden as Johanna Maria Lind. Her family was poor, but when Jenny was only nine years old, she was given the opportunity to attend the Royal Theater in Stockholm as a voice student. At the age of seventeen, she appeared in her first opera, and at the age of twenty-one, she studied in Paris under the famous Spanish singer Manuel García. About her training she wrote, "What I most wanted to know was two or three things and with those he did help me. The rest I knew myself, and the birds and our Lord as the maestro [teacher] did the rest."

Word of Jenny's incredible talent spread quickly. Composers, including the famous Giuseppe Verdi, began writing parts specifically for her. Crowds were going crazy for her, and she was nicknamed the Swedish Nightingale.

Despite the popularity, Jenny's opera career was short-lived because she retired when her mother and a clergyman convinced her that opera was evil. On Jenny's last appearance, Queen Victoria was in attendance. The Queen later wrote in her diary, "The great event of the evening was Jenny Lind's appearance and her complete triumph.

She has a most exquisite, powerful, and really quite peculiar voice, so round, soft, and flexible."

Instead of singing opera, Jenny now wanted to focus on her faith. She also wanted to become a solo performer. However, before she could fully develop those plans, show promoter P. T. Barnum invited her to tour the United States under his guidance. Although he had never heard her voice, Barnum recognized the value of her popularity in Europe. He promised her a huge salary and 150 shows. Considering the large amount that she could donate to charity, which she did quite often throughout her career, Jenny agreed.

Jenny didn't allow her popularity to weaken her faith in God or her desire to help people in need.

The larger-than-life showman whipped up a frenzy among Americans to attend Jenny's shows. He placed ads in the paper, held auctions for tickets, and created such an interest that by the time she made it to New York, a crowd of over thirty thousand was waiting to cheer her arrival. None of them had even heard her sing before!

But America loved her! She sold out shows, setting box office records. Fans bought up anything Lind-related, including women's hats, opera glasses, and paper dolls. Jenny avoided heavy makeup and overly fashionable outfits, and her audiences loved her simple innocence. They were impressed that Jenny donated thousands of dollars to charities along her tour. A newspaper article once explained that it was not her voice or her beauty that made her so popular but her kindness and her faith in God. It said, "It is her high moral character—her spotless name, which the breath of slander has never tainted—her benevolence—her charity—her amiable temper—the religious sentiment which she so carefully cultivates." Jenny didn't allow her popularity to weaken her faith in God or her desire to help people in need.

The US tour lasted around twenty months. Toward the end of it, Jenny married her accompanist, Otto Goldschmidt. When she returned to Sweden, she used some of her earnings to start a music academy for girls. Jenny and Otto later made their home in Germany and England and had three children. For about thirty years, Jenny didn't sing regularly, but she occasionally performed at charity events. She also spent a few years teaching at London's Royal College of Music. About her singing, she once said, "I do like to sing to God!"

She died at the age of sixty-seven.

Jenny inspires us to recognize that God is the giver of our talents and to be thankful for His gifts.

PRAYER

Dear God, thank You for Jenny Lind's example of faithful and humble service. Help me use my gifts in a way that brings You joy. Amen.

ANNE BRADSTREET

Poet (1612–1672)

Writing from the Heart

Have you ever had to move to a new place—perhaps a new home, a new city, a new state, or a new country? Imagine leaving your home and traveling to a new land on the other side of the sea in order to worship God the way you and the members of your church group wanted to. Imagine going to a place that was still mostly wilderness and having to trust God for all things. Anne Bradstreet traveled to America when it was a new country, and she wrote poems to talk about God and describe the world around her.

Anne was born in England into a wealthy family. Because her father was in charge of the property of a nobleman, Anne grew up in a castle. Her family was part of a religious group called the Puritans, who were devout Christians that wanted to improve the church in England. As a young girl, Anne was very aware of her relationship with God and enjoyed reading the Bible. She wrote, "I . . . found much comfort in reading the Scriptures."

At age sixteen, Anne married Simon Bradstreet, the son of a Puritan minister. It was shortly after her marriage that Anne's father, her husband, and some leaders of the Puritans made plans to take their families to America and settle in the Massachusetts Bay area. They were hoping to build a community where they could live their Puritan lifestyle in peace.

The trip to America took seventy-two days. Imagine being stuck on a boat—often in stormy weather, tossed to and fro—and not seeing land for two and a half months! What a joy they must have felt when they finally saw land. However, the conditions of the colony that they were traveling to were very poor, so the group eventually traveled to another area to set up their new settlement.

These sudden changes were difficult for Anne. In two short years she went from being a child to a married woman. She left a life of luxury for a life of hardship. She left the established country of England for the unknowns of the new frontier. The situation tested Anne's faith, but in the end she knew she was following God's plan for her life.

"I have had great experience of God's hearing my prayers."

Anne started writing two years after arriving in America. She would write about her life: her joys, her sorrows, and her love for God, her husband, and her children. On one occasion, she wrote this poem about her children:

I had eight birds hatched in one nest,
Four Cocks there were, and Hens the rest,
I nursed them up with pain and care,
Nor cost, nor labor did I spare,
Till at the last they felt their wing,
Mounted the Trees, and learned to sing.

Her husband was often away on business, and she missed him dearly. She wrote, "To My Dear and Loving Husband," which included such lines as the following:

If ever two were one, then surely we.
If ever man were loved by wife, then thee.
If ever wife was happy in a man,
Compare with me, ye women, if you can.

Without Anne's knowledge, her brother-in-law took some of her poems to England, where they were published in a collection titled *The Tenth Muse Lately Sprung Up in America*. It was the only publication of her poems during her lifetime, making her one of the first published American poets. She became more popular many years after her death, and she is now among the most popular historic poets of the United States.

Anne's health suffered from time to time, and life, with its unexpected troubles, sometimes brought her pain and sorrow. But she found comfort through prayer. She wrote, "I have had great experience of God's hearing my prayers, and returning comfortable answers to me, either in granting the thing I prayed for, or else in satisfying my mind without it."

She died after a long illness at sixty years of age.

Anne inspires us to acknowledge God in all things and to seek His comfort always.

PRAYER

Dear God, the life You have given me is precious. Help me to see the world through Your eyes and to please You with my life. Amen.

CORRIE TEN BOOM
Holocaust Survivor, Evangelist (1892–1983)
A Faithful Witness for God

Can you trust God, even in the darkest of situations? Do you know that He can bring light out of darkness and hope out of despair? Corrie ten Boom experienced God's love in amazing ways and obediently spread His message of hope throughout the world.

Corrie was born in the Netherlands to a family that loved Jesus very much. Each morning, Corrie's father would read from their large Bible, and the family often had Bible studies in their home. They also lived out their faith by helping the poor, opening their home to people who needed a meal or to missionary children who needed a home, and treating all people with love.

When Corrie was thirty-two, she became the first woman in Holland to work as a licensed watchmaker. She worked alongside her father and his other helpers in the small shop that was attached to their home. Corrie also ran a Christian girls club for fifteen years. Her family had a busy but peaceful life. But everything changed with the start of World War II.

Adolf Hitler and his Nazi army invaded many countries in Europe. When Corrie was forty-eight, they invaded Holland. Groups like her Christian girls club were shut down, and Jews lost their privileges since the Nazis hated Jews. Some of Corrie's relatives joined the resistance, a group that worked secretly to stop the Nazis. Corrie began communicating with resistance workers using her father's shop as a cover since people came in and out to do business. She, her sister

Betsie, and her father knew they had to do something to protect the Jews from the evil that was happening.

Corrie and her father had a small, secret room built behind a false wall in Corrie's bedroom. There they could hide Jews and resistance workers if needed. Over the years, Corrie and her family helped save about eight hundred lives.

One afternoon, the German secret police received a tip and raided their home. Thankfully, they didn't find the six people who were hiding in the small room. However, they arrested Corrie, some family members, and several others who were at the house for a prayer meeting.

Over the years, Corrie and her family helped save about eight hundred lives.

Everyone except Corrie, Betsie, and their father was quickly released. Their father died ten days later in prison. Eventually, the sisters were sent to a prison camp in the Netherlands. They were later taken into Germany and placed in the Ravensbrück concentration camp.

Through a miracle, the sisters smuggled a Bible into the camp. They would read from it with their fellow prisoners. Many people came to know Jesus. Corrie struggled in loving her enemies—the guards—like the Bible says to. Betsie, however, set an example of selflessness, love, and forgiveness. Corrie later recalled, "I saw a gray uniform and a visored hat; Betsie saw a wounded human being."

Betsie, who was seven years older than Corrie, had been in poor health. She died after three months in Ravensbrück. Days later, Corrie was miraculously released! A week later, all the women her age at the camp were killed. Corrie joined her surviving family members in the

Netherlands. Inspired by Betsie, she established a home for those recovering from the horrors of the camps, and she preached the need for forgiveness.

One day Corrie came face to face with a Ravensbrück guard. He had become a Christian and had accepted God's forgiveness for what he had done during the war. He asked Corrie for her forgiveness. She froze. She didn't think she could forgive him, but she knew she had to. She prayed for Jesus to help her. Then, Corrie reached out to take the man's hand and offered her forgiveness. She later wrote, "When He tells us to love our enemies, He gives, along with the command, the love itself." How amazing our God is!

Corrie died on her ninety-first birthday.

Corrie inspires us to trust God's love for us and to praise Him with our lives.

PRAYER

Dear God, help me, like Corrie ten Boom, to see Your faithfulness in all situations and to share Your love with all people. Amen.

ABIGAIL ADAMS
First Lady (1744–1818)
Leading from Behind the Scenes

Can you imagine what it must have been like to live over two hundred years ago in the newly created United States? At that time, men were in charge. They called all the shots, made all the decisions, and decided how the government should be run. In fact, women didn't even earn the right to vote until 1919—that's 143 years after the country began! But peeking behind the curtain of American history, you'll find there were many important women influencing America's forefathers all along. Abigail Adams was one of these amazing women.

Abigail married her husband, John Adams, at the age of nineteen, and both went on to influence America for many years. While most women in the 1700s focused on raising a family, Abigail dedicated her life to not only raising a great family but also shaping a great country. Because John spent so much time away from home for political meetings, Abigail and John wrote each other over one thousand letters.

Since Abigail never went to school, she put in the hard work of learning to read and write at home. While Abigail's letters were full of encouragement for her husband and updates on the children, her thoughts didn't stop there. Many of her letters to John were also filled with her political hopes and dreams. Even though being a deep thinker was not something people expected of women at this time, Abigail used the mind God gave her for good.

She once wrote, "Learning is not attained by chance, it must be sought for with ardor and attended to with diligence." "Sought for with ardor" means to chase after something with passion and excitement. Think of the opportunities God has put in front of you. Do you go after those things with joy and anticipation of what God will do with your talents? "Attended to with diligence" means to continue working on your abilities and skills with faithful, hard work. Think of something in your own life that you want to seek after passionately and give your time and attention to. Is it relationships with siblings? School work? Spending time with Jesus?

Abigail lived with wisdom from God and fought for kind and equal treatment of all people.

One way that God blessed Abigail's efforts was through her children. Abigail realized her greatest contribution to the country might be not something she said or did but *someone* she raised. She believed her role as a mother was to prepare her children to be good citizens and political participants. Amazingly, one of her sons eventually became president!

Abigail was not only a dedicated learner, writer, and mother; she also served as a vital confidant and adviser to her husband. Right after John became president in 1797, he wrote to her, "I have never wanted your advice and assistance more in my life." Abigail influenced the way her husband thought and made decisions. Abigail lived with wisdom from God and fought for kind and equal treatment of all people.

In one of her most famous letters, she urged John to "remember the ladies." Long before women had earned the right to vote, Abigail knew that God had created men and women as equals and given women a unique perspective that deserved to be heard. By speaking her mind, Abigail began conversations about the way women were treated that set a new course for the country.

Abigail Adams lived a life full of thoughtful decisions, strong opinions, and quiet humility. Throughout her life, she supported her husband well, cared for her children faithfully, and never stopped showing an interest and passion for the American nation. Look at what God has put in your life. How could you live your life in a way that honors God by working hard with a kind heart and humble attitude? Abigail Adams embodied a spirit of dedication, spunk, and love for God that came out in her love for her family and her country.

PRAYER

Dear God, thank You for Abigail Adams. Thank You for the way she shows me how to work hard to accomplish things that seem impossible for me. Thank You that You have given me unique gifts. Help me discover them and use them to help people see You. Amen.

FLANNERY O'CONNOR
Author (1925–1964)
Devoted Storyteller

Did you know that before phones and computers were widely used, people sent urgent messages long-distance over the telegraph? Electrical signals were sent to telegraph stations, where a message was taken and then delivered to a person. Sometimes people needed a very important message delivered, and the telegraph was the fastest way. Flannery O'Connor had an important message that she delivered in her writings. She wrote of the need of people to recognize God's great love for them.

Flannery was born to a wealthy and well-respected family in Savannah, Georgia. Her parents were strong, practicing Catholics, and as the only child, she willingly followed her parents' example. During Flannery's youth, her father suffered from a disease called lupus erythematosus, where one's own body starts attacking the healthy parts of the body. This forced the family to move to a small rural town. Here, she enjoyed birds and raising chickens.

When Flannery was fifteen, her father died. To stay close to home, she attended a nearby women's college. Flannery became the editor of the college's literary magazine, contributing various writings and humorous cartoons. During her college years, Flannery's writing started to get noticed, especially when she became part of the Writer's Workshop program at the University of Iowa for her master's degree. However, she hated speaking in front of people, so her professor would read her stories to the group at the workshop.

When Flannery was twenty-five, she developed the same disease as her father. In constant pain and exhaustion, she was forced to return to the family's Georgia farm, where her mother cared for her. How frustrating that must have been! In the midst of becoming a promising writer, she had to deal with a disease that would eventually take her life.

Despite her illness, Flannery spent two hours each day at her typewriter to work on her stories and essays. She also wrote a number of letters to friends, helped raise peacocks on the farm, and attended Mass at the local Catholic Church every day. The result of her writing was an impressive collection of short stories, novels, letters, and book reviews.

Flannery understood how great God is and how much we need Him!

Flannery's stories were not sweet, heartwarming tales. She created characters who struggled with their faith in God and suffered through a variety of situations so they could understand their need for God's love and forgiveness. Perhaps because of her disease, she knew her own life was precious, and she wanted others to receive God's love. She also said, "A story is a way to say something that can't be said any other way, and it takes every word in the story to say what the meaning is."

A prayer journal published after Flannery's death gives insight into her relationship with God. One entry, written while she was in college, tells of her desire to know God better. She wrote, "Dear God, I cannot love Thee the way I want to. You are the slim crescent of a moon that I see and my self is the earth's shadow that keeps me from seeing all the moon." She also wrote, "I measure God by everything I'm not." Flannery understood how great God is and how much we need Him!

Toward the end of Flannery's short life, lupus made it difficult for her to walk, but she still faithfully went to church every day. When she was finally admitted to the hospital, Flannery kept her writing under her pillow so the doctors wouldn't take it away. Flannery's dedication to her writing provides an inspirational example of using the gifts that God gives us despite the trials in our lives.

She died at the age of thirty-nine.

Flannery inspires us to be willing to commit ourselves to telling people about our faith in God whether we are healthy or sick.

PRAYER

Dear God, although Flannery lived a very short life, she lived it to the full. Help me use each day I have as an opportunity to love and serve You. Amen.

References

Mother Teresa: Biography.com editors. 2014. "Mother Teresa Biography." Biography.com. Last updated June 19, 2019. https://www.biography.com/people/mother-teresa-9504160.

Irena Sendler: AZ Quotes. n.d. "Irena Sendler Quotes." AZQuotes.com. Accessed June 24, 2019. https://www.azquotes.com/author/30375-Irena_Sendler.

Sendler, Irena. Interview in *Irena Sendler: In the Name of Their Mothers* (documentary), directed by John Kent Harrison. Released May 1, 2011. New York: Public Broadcasting Service.

Lise Meitner: Sime, Ruth Lewin. 1996. *Lise Meitner: A Life in Physics*. Los Angeles: University of California Press, 354, 379.

Rosa Parks: "Rosa Parks and the Bus Ride That Changed America." 2010. Christianity.com. https://www.christianity.com/church/church-history/church-history-for-kids/rosa-parks-and-the-bus-ride-that-changed-america-11635083.html.

Lottie Moon: Platt, David. 2018. "Lottie Moon: The Long Shadow of a Tiny Missionary Giant." International Mission Board. https://www.imb.org/2018/07/23/lottie-moon-story/.

Wilma Rudolph: Black History in America. n.d. "Wilma Rudolph." Myblackhistory.net. Accessed June 24, 2019. http://www.myblackhistory.net/Wilma_Rudolph.htm.

White, David. n.d. "Wilma Rudolph: A Story of Determination." SocialStudiesforkids.com. Accessed, April 30, 2019. http://www.socialstudiesforkids.com/articles/ushistory/wilmarudolph.htm.

Lucy Jane Rider Meyer: Brown, Irva Colley. 1985. "In Their Time: A History of the Chicago Training School on the Occasion of Its Centennial Celebration 1885–1985." Chicago Training School Records (Garrett-Evangelical Theological Seminary), 27. http://collections.carli.illinois.edu/cdm/compoundobject/collection/uni_cts/id/50/rec/1.

Fanny Crosby: Christianity.com staff. 2010. "Fanny Crosby: America's Hymn Queen." Christianity.com. https://www.christianity.com/church/church-history/timeline/1801-1900/fanny-crosby-americas-hymn-queen-11630385.html.

Jeanette Li: Doyle, Frances. n.d. "Jeanette Li." Biographical Dictionary of Chinese Christianity online. Accessed June 24, 2019. http://bdcconline.net/en/stories/li-jeanette.

Mary Kay Ash: "Celebrating Mary Kay Ash: Her Wisdom—Faith," Marykaytribute.com. Accessed June 24, 2019. http://www.marykaytribute.com/wisdomfaith.aspx.

Amy Carmichael: Carmichael, Amy, and Judith Couchman. 1996. *A Very Present Help*. Ann Arbor, MI: Vine Books.

Sophia Jex-Blake: McCullins, Darren. 2018. "Sophia Jex-Blake: The Battle to Be Scotland's First Female Doctor." BBC Scotland. https://www.bbc.com/news/uk-scotland-edinburgh-east-fife-46180368.

Madeleine L'Engle: Biography.com editors. 2014. "Madeleine L'Engle Biography." Biography.com. Last updated April 16, 2019. https://www.biography.com/people/madeleine-lengle-9378983.

Mattingly, Terry. 2007. "Tesser Well, Madeleine L'Engle." *Terry Mattingly: On Religion* (blog). Patheos.com. https://www.patheos.com/blogs/tmatt/2007/09/tesser-well-madeleine-lengle/.

Kayla Mueller: Kayla's Hands. n.d. Accessed June 27, 2019. http://kaylashands.org/.

Walker, Tim. 2015. "ISIS Hostage: How Is Kayla Mueller?" *Independent*. https://www.independent.co.uk/news/world/americas/isis-hostage-who-is-kayla-mueller-10036525.html.

Jenny Lind: America's Story from America's Library. n.d. "Jenny Lind." Americaslibrary.gov. Accessed June 27, 2019. http://www.americaslibrary.gov/aa/lind/aa_lind_subj.html.

Emerson, Isabelle Putnam. 2005. *Five Centuries of Women Singers*. Westport, CT: Praeger.

The Lost Museum Archive. "Jenny Lind: The Secret of Her Popularity—Her Movements Yesterday." *New York Herald*, September 6, 1850. American Social History Productions, Inc. Accessed June 27, 2019. https://lostmuseum.cuny.edu/archive/jenny-lindthe-secret-of-her-popularityher.

Corrie ten Boom: Guideposts. 2014. "Guideposts Classics: Corrie ten Boom on Forgiveness." Originally published November 1972. Guideposts.org. https://www.guideposts.org/better-living/positive-living/guideposts-classics-corrie-ten-boom-on-forgiveness.

McDaniel, Debbie. 2016. "10 Amazing Things You Never Knew about Corrie ten Boom." Crosswalk.com. https://www.crosswalk.com/faith/women/10-amazing-things-you-never-knew-about-corrie-ten-boom.html.

Ten Boom, Corrie. 1958. *Not Good if Detached*. London: Christian Literature Crusade.

Flannery O'Connor: Goodreads. "Flannery O'Connor Quotes" n.d. Goodreads.com. Accessed June 27, 2019. https://www.goodreads.com/author/quotes/22694.Flannery_O_Connor.

Marsh, Karen Wright. 2017. "The Demanding Faith of Flannery O'Connor." *Christianity Today*. https://www.christianitytoday.com/women/2017/september/demanding-faith-flannery-oconnor.html.

Taylor, Justin. 2013. "Flannery O'Connor Reads 'A Good Man Is Hard to Find'" (blog post). The Gospel Coalition. https://www.thegospelcoalition.org/blogs/justin-taylor/flannery-oconnor-reads-a-good-man-is-hard-to-find/.

LIVE YOUR FAITH

Dear Friend,

This book was prayerfully crafted with you, the reader, in mind—every word, every sentence, every page—was thoughtfully written, designed, and packaged to encourage you...right where you are this very moment. At DaySpring, our vision is to see every person experience the life-changing message of God's love. So, as we worked through rough drafts, design changes, edits and details, we prayed for you to deeply experience His unfailing love, indescribable peace, and pure joy. It is our sincere hope that through these Truth-filled pages your heart will be blessed, knowing that God cares about you—your desires and disappointments, your challenges and dreams.

He knows. He cares. He loves you unconditionally.

BLESSINGS!
THE DAYSPRING BOOK TEAM

Additional copies of this book and
other DaySpring titles can be purchased
at fine bookstores everywhere.
Order online at dayspring.com
or
by phone at 1-877-751-4347